Fifty Years of UTV

Fifty 50 Years of UTV

Don Anderson
Gill & Macmillan

Gill & Macmillan

Gill & Macmillan Ltd
Hume Avenue, Park West, Dublin 12
with associated companies throughout the world
www.gillmacmillan.ie

© Don Anderson 2009
978 07171 4454 9

Index compiled by Verba Editing House
Design and print origination by Design Image
Printed in Great Britain by Butler Tanner & Dennis

This book is typeset in 10.5 Berling Roman on 18 point.

A CIP catalogue record for this book is available from the British Library.

1 3 5 4 2

Contents

Preface

The activity of some companies and industries is so interwoven with everyday life that an account of what they have done can define elements of a society. There are many examples. On the world stage, plucked with serendipitous randomness, are Microsoft and Boeing; in the UK and Ireland, Guinness, the canal and rail networks and even fish and chips; in Belfast and Northern Ireland, Harland and Wolff and the linen industry.

Also for Ireland, Northern Ireland, Belfast and even the UK, in that category I nominate Ulster Television, or UTV, as commonly known even from before its first transmission. (I have used UTV and Ulster Television indiscriminately, though the company only adopted UTV officially as its name relatively late in the day.)

UTV has been narrating and illustrating the fortunes of Northern Ireland, good and bad, during an extraordinary half-century. In that time we have been through a revolution, both literally and metaphorically. Dwell upon some of the happenings and processes – among them, the Troubles; the *rapprochement* of London and Dublin; the fall and rise of Stormont; the decline of the old smokestack industries; the European project which made the Irish border invisible on the landscape; easy international travel; mobile phones and the electronic revolution; commercial activity in space, including the transmission of UTV's programmes; the internet; global warming and global terrorism. These and other happenings have changed our society to the point where the world of 1959 can seem almost as distant as that of 1859. UTV has been part of that process and an incremental chronicler of it. In these pages I have sought to illustrate that fact.

This, therefore, is not a compendium of programmes, some of which would be half or entirely forgotten. As someone who worked in the broadcasting business, both BBC and commercial, and in newspapers, I know just how ephemeral television programmes are. Notwithstanding the advent of 'catch-up' TV on the internet, a programme from UTV broadcast on the day you read this became history with its closing credits. A baguette, even a newspaper or ice cream, can have a longer shelf life.

But the avalanche of programmes on practically every aspect of our common existence issued from UTV has had an impact, sometimes shatteringly so. One need only think of the documentary, 'Suffer Little Children', and its sequel, to make the point. The Roman Catholic Church and Irish society are still reverberating from the consequences and fallout of the revelation of abuse activities behind the Church's walls. However, it is in the constant coverage of the more commonplace, in its entertainments and in its advertisements that UTV has had the most significant impact. Because of that, it nearly seamlessly became part of daily existence in Northern Ireland.

It is also not insignificant that Ulster Television is one of the few companies to survive independently from the formation in the 1950s of commercial television in the United Kingdom. That was due in part to an accident of geography, in part to the exploitation of geography, but also in major part to an astute direction of its affairs. It means that UTV has travelled from being an ITV company, regarding which there were initial fears about viability, to one of the very few ITV companies not swallowed up by ITV plc and which is standing steadily on its own feet with every prospect of continuing to do so. But then, UTV always punched above its weight in the ITV system.

There are many inside and outside the company who helped me put this account together and I am grateful to them all, particularly Orla McKibben, head of communications and Janice Freeland, personal assistant to group chief executive John McCann. The list also includes, in no particular order: JB McGuckian, John McCann, Sinead Doyle, Michael Beattie, Brian Black, Alan Bremner, Adrienne Catherwood, Eric Caves, Courtney Hutchinson, Paul Hutchinson, Jim Creagh, Liam Creagh, Gordon Duffield, Joel Simon, Alan McFarland, David Lyle, Helen Madden, Derek Martin, Rob Morrison, Brian Owens, John Rosborough, Ian Sanderson, Brian Waddell, Robin Walsh, Iain Webster, Andy Wood, Moore Sinnerton, Shauna Melanaphy, Carmel Mullen and Tony Fleck.

I had the goodwill of the company management, but I think I can venture that this account is not the book they would have commissioned. While it contains overwhelmingly a constructive and indeed affectionate account of how UTV got where it is today, there is material in these pages that the company might have wished forgotten. So this is very much my own view of UTV and its contribution to wider society. The opinions and conclusions in this book, its selections and omissions, are to be laid at my door, not at that of UTV.

I make special mention of Robert Lamrock, channel development manager of UTV. Among his responsibilities is that of the UTV archive and image library. In the library, Robert oversees an extremely valuable historical resource, consisting mainly of film and tapes of events big and small. The collection is now so large and so important that I believe some means of channelling public money as a contribution to its upkeep should be devised and agreed. Of course, the collection belongs to UTV, but in a very real sense it belongs to all of us, for it is a unique record of half a century of Northern Ireland's history and heritage. The burden of maintaining it should be shared. In the meantime, it is on the shoulders of UTV and Robert. Luckily for all of us, Robert has the soul and intellect of an historian and archivist.

And while on the subject of historical collections, the archive housed at the Ulster Folk and Transport Museum at Cultra near Belfast was of great value. My thanks go to my former colleague in broadcasting, Tim Cooke, now Chief Executive of National Museums Northern Ireland, to Clifford Harkness, Head of Collections Management, George Dixon, librarian, and photographers George Wright and Alan McCartney. Wonderful, helpful people working in yet another most valuable cultural store bursting at the seams.

And finally I doff my cap to Fergal Tobin, Publishing Director of Gill & Macmillan, to Deirdre Rennison Kunz, Helen Thompson and Nicki Howard. They perform magic on a word-processed document. Doubtless they are all thankful that books have a greater shelf life than TV programmes and that television and other technologies have not yet managed to overtake the tome, try as they will.

Don Anderson
Newtownards, June 2009

Timeline

YEAR	UTV & UTV RELATED HISTORY	TV & CONTEXT HISTORY
1953		First TV pictures for Northern Ireland from the Glencairn transmitter, beaming BBC. Glencairn was a temporary transmitter replaced by Divis. The final year of sales of 9-inch sets coincides with the beginning of sales of 17-inch sets.
1954	The establishment of the ITA paves the way for consortia and groups to apply as programme contractors for Northern Ireland. In the original system, the ITA owned the independent TV transmitters and contracted various companies in UK regions to supply the programmes. The regions co-operated to provide programmes to serve as a network, leaving 'holes' for local programmes.	Independent Television Authority (ITA) established as a public corporation to oversee and regulate new independent television to provide competition to BBC. World's first regular colour TV service begins in America. TV licence raised from £2 to £3, first increase since its introduction in 1946. The first live weather report broadcast.
1955	Independent television begins in London but must wait for the formation of UTV to reach Northern Ireland. Television comes to Northern Ireland in the form of a single BBC channel, relayed from Kirk o'Shotts in Scotland.	Start of Independent Television in London area by Associated-Rediffusion and Associated Television, together with the non-profit-making Independent Television News. First TV advertisement is for Gibbs SR toothpaste. Estimated number of viewers in the UK now exceeding twelve million.
1956		Independent Television begins to spread beyond London and southeast England. Armchair Theatre (ABC) begins. A Nielsen survey revealed that of the programmes in the top ten ratings, three quarters were commercial. Philco introduce the first full-functioned remote.
1957		'Emergency Ward 10' (ATV). First regular schools programming on Associated Rediffusion. Commercial Scottish Television company begins.
1958	Ulster Television wins the Independent Television Authority contract to provide programmes to the ITA Northern Ireland transmitters. Buys Havelock House and an adjoining property on the Ormeau Road, Belfast.	The 17" CRT now clearly seen as the minimum standard for new televisions. Associated-Rediffusion shows first programme from an Ampex video tape recorder, which becomes the established format for recording and playback. TV households exceed radio-only households for the first time. Introduction of push-button TV tuning by the Bush set manufacturers.
1959	Ulster Television begins the ITV service for Northern Ireland from Black Mountain above Belfast at 4.45 p.m. on 31 Oct. Two days later 'Roundabout' begins with Anne Gregg & Ivor Mills. Estimated 97,000 viewers in NI. Film Producer Bill MacQuitty is managing director. Subsidiary company Ulster Television Publications Ltd formed to publish *TV Post* listing guide. The station's first on-screen logo was an oscilloscope pattern made up of seven dots joined together by six lines. The logo animated to a jingle based on the local folk tune 'The Mountains of Mourne'.	Tyne Tees begins providing the ITV service for the northeast of England. Anglia Television begins the ITV service for the east of England from the Mendelsham transmitter, at the time the highest mast (1,000 ft) in Europe. ITV now covers 90 per cent of the UK population. 10 million TV licences. Purchase (sales) tax on televisions and radios reduced from 60 per cent to 50 per cent.
1960	2,500 local people have appeared on screen.	'Coronation Street' soap by Granada begins.

YEAR	UTV & UTV RELATED HISTORY	TV & CONTEXT HISTORY
1961	Bruce Forsythe appears in 'Roundabout'. Nightly Episodes. Television advertising taxed. UTV ad revenue reaches £1 million. UTV now assisting training at other new TV companies.	Natural history landmark series 'Survival' begins (Anglia). RTÉ begins TV transmissions 31 December.
1962	New extension to Havelock House containing new studio. Daily UTV news service introduced. 'Midnight Oil', groundbreaking forty-two part educational series, on UTV. Total homes in NI receiving UTV doubled from 1959, to 200,000. Revenue down 5 per cent due to credit squeeze.	First video tape slow-motion replay. Pilkington Report published, recommending the restructuring of ITV, a second BBC channel, a separate BBC service for Wales, change of line standard from 405 to 625 lines and colour on 625-line UHF. First transatlantic satellite TV broadcast.
1963	Coverage of UTV spreads to western parts of Northern Ireland when the Strabane transmitter opens in February 1963. Five local programmes in the regional top ten in one week. UTV first company to mount tribute programme to assassinated President Kennedy. 'Teatime with Tommy' begins.	Television Act 1963 provides for the start of BBC2.
1964	UTV reappointed as programme contractor for Northern Ireland. London sales offices in Marylebone Road acquired. Brum Henderson appointed to the new ITN to represent five of the ITV companies, all of whom jointly own ITN.	All ITV contractors reappointed. Wales West and North (WWN) fails – the only ITV company ever to do so. Taken over by Television Wales and West (TWW). Television Act includes code of advertising standards and combines 1954 and 1963 Acts. Mary Whitehouse establishes the 'Clean Up TV' campaign, later the National Viewers' and Listeners' Association (NVLA) and now Mediawatch-UK.
1965	A first in Irish broadcasting history when 'Parade', the UTV nightly magazine programme, links Belfast with Belfast, Maine, USA via the Early Bird telecommunications satellite.	Ban on cigarette advertising on television. Significant network programme: 'Peyton Place', the first prime-time soap.
1966	First UTV marketing guide to Northern Ireland published. 'The Orange and the Green', UTV documentary, shown widely over the network. UTV underwrites the 1966 Grand Opera House season in Belfast with a deficiency guarantee of £1,000.	British Bureau of Television Advertising formed, with UTV Sales Director, MR Hutcheson as one of the directors.
1967	UTV programme contract with the ITA renewed for a further six years. UTV's first one-hour drama, 'Boatman Do Not Tarry', written by John D. Stewart. 'Flashpoint', from the newly formed current affairs unit, begins as a late evening current affairs programme.	All ITV contracts extended until 1968. First 'News at Ten'. Northern Ireland's first colour TV transmissions (BBC2). Significant network programme: 'The Prisoner' (ATV).
1968	*TV Post*, UTV's programme guide, published by the company, ceases, as a regional edition of the national *TV Times* takes over. 'Boatman Do Not Tarry' is broadcast nationally over the ITV network. Late night music series 'An Evening With . . .', 'Profile' series, 'By This I Live' and traditional music 'From Glen to Glen'. Capt. Terence O'Neill & Eddie McAteer in historic broadcast together on religious programme, 'The Land We Love'. Religious programme 'Face of the Waters' networked & wins certificate at the Monte Carlo festival. Second UTV marketing guide.	ITV franchise changes take effect. New ITV contracts take effect: LWT replaces ATV London; Yorkshire TV forms new region from part of old Granada area, Harlech replaces TWW; Thames formed by ABC and Rediffusion. ATV takes on all-week midlands franchise. Granada takes on all-week northwest franchise. Technician strike takes the network off air.
1969	1969 generally taken as the date for the start of the Troubles. TV advertising levy increased, prompting UTV to set aside plans for a new colour studio complex on the banks of the Lagan. UTV completely converted from old 405-line standard to 625-line.	ITV goes colour, using the PAL 625-line system on UHF in England, Scotland & Wales. Live pictures of men on the Moon.

YEAR	UTV & UTV RELATED HISTORY	TV & CONTEXT HISTORY
	'UTV Reports', daily news magazine. 'The Crusades', adult education series, 'What's It All About'. 'Seven Degrees West', series concentrating on matters outside Belfast. 'It's All Happening', 75-min peak-time current affairs series. First logo redesign, which runs to 1993. Now reaching 335,000 NI homes.	
1970	UHF PAL colour service launched with the opening of the UHF transmitter on Divis Mtn. 90 per cent of UTV output available in colour. New equipment includes colour film processing. 'No Surrender', colour documentary on the Twelfth (partly networked); 'Let's Look at Ulster', schools series; 'Sportscast', preview on Friday evenings; 'Take Time with Tommy' introducing new musical talent. And 'Tommy's Tavern', old-time music hall style show.	
1971	'Deadline', current affairs programme. 'Sounds Like McEvoy', music. 'Sporting Challenge', sports quiz. 'Spectrum', the creative scene. 'Johnny', story of a travelling man. Leaders of the four main churches in a discussion programme about the Troubles. Second colour telecine and two TR70C VTRs installed. Advertising revenue reaches £1.5 million.	Significant network programme: 'Upstairs Downstairs' (LWT).
1972	New central and master control rooms in the extension of Havelock House. Studio colour introduced. De-restriction on hours of broadcast. TV receiver set count stands at 360,000. Sydney Perry appointed programme controller. Considerable news footage now being broadcast from UTV for ITN because of the Troubles.	ITA becomes IBA and strengthens control and supervision of ITV companies. Removal of restrictions on broadcasting hours. Significant network programme: 'Weekend World' (LWT). IBA engineers demonstrate the world's first digital converter for changing pictures from the US 525-line format into the 625-line European standard.
1973	Saturday night 'Gordon Burns Hour', with Irish broadcasting first live programming link between Belfast and Dublin. New film library. £350,000 earmarked to complete colourisation, total expenditure being £0.5 million. Exclusive interview with the Prime Minister, Edward Heath, at 10 Downing St. Assembly and local council election broadcasts. Evidence submitted to the Crawford Committee on television coverage. Second colour film processing line installed. Revenue jumps by 20 per cent.	Independent Broadcasting Authority Act consolidates 1964 Television Act and 1972 Sound Broadcasting Act. Significant network programme: 'Within These Walls' (LWT).
1974	No interruption of service during the UWC strike, which brings down the first Unionist/SDLP power-sharing Stormont government. 2,000th edition of 'Romper Room'. 'Look Ahead', 13-part adult education series with Queen's University. Mk8 telecine and vision mixer installed in Studio 1.	All ITV contracts renewed until 1976. Video cassette recorders go on sale. Life of IBA extended to 1979. IBA changes basis of Exchequer levy from ad revenue to profits. Oracle teletext introduced for ITV. Slump in stock markets.
1975	'Lunchtime', mini-magazine midday programme. Lord Aylestone, outgoing chair of the IBA, and his successor, Lady Plowden, visit the station. Third UTV marketing guide published. Limavady UHF transmitter opened. Evidence submitted to the Annan Committee on Broadcasting. 'The Economic Case', special four-part series with politicians and economists on the economic options for trouble-torn Northern Ireland. Annan Committee evidence from UTV published.	Lady Plowden becomes Chairman of the IBA. First regular teletext broadcasts. Significant network programme: 'The Naked Civil Servant' (Thames TV). The findings of the Crawford Committee on Broadcasting Coverage include the recommendation that the duplication of VHF 405-line services by UHF 625-line transmissions should be completed as soon after 1980 as possible, to release VHF bands for re-allocation. The Annan Committee on the Future of Broadcasting received submissions from interested parties.

YEAR	UTV & UTV RELATED HISTORY	TV & CONTEXT HISTORY
1976	New contract with the IBA to supply programmes for Ulster until 1979. Brian Waddell in control of local programmes. Sir Brian Young, director general of the IBA, visits Havelock House. UTV sponsors the 'Hobbies and Holidays' exhibition at the King's Hall. 'Salute to America' week, celebrating the bicentenary of the USA and visit of the American ambassador, Anne Armstrong.	ITV's twenty-first anniversary. Colour sets outnumber monochrome sets for the first time in the UK. Wage agreement settles on 20 per cent rise in the industry. Prestigious Faraday Lecture at Queen's University on television technology from Howard Steele and Boris Townsend of the Independent Broadcasting Authority. All ITV contracts renewed until 1979.
1977	Silver jubilee visit by the Queen, and UTV's first major outside broadcast. Major documentary, 'Ulster – The Right to Strike', networked nationally. Derek Murray in London for 'Murray's London' weekly series. Tribute and funeral coverage of Cardinal Conway. Three-hour outside broadcast of the ordination of Archbishop Tomás Ó Fiaich. Four studio specials, 'Faces of Violence', 'Away From It All', 'Irish History-Reality' and 'Myth and Energy for Ulster'. School series, 'Hop, Skip & Jump' for seven-year-olds. Limavady and Londonderry transmitters commissioned. Lord Antrim, first chairman, dies. Succeeded by James MacQuitty, brother of Bill.	Annan Report on the Future of Broadcasting recommends setting up Broadcast Complaints Commission and a joint BBC/ITV audience measurement system. It also recommends a fourth channel, to be regulated by a new body.
1978	'Ulster Reports', local news programme. 'When Irish Stars are Shining', 60-min St Patrick's Day special, networked. Five programmes from Balmoral Show Grounds. Networked documentary, 'The Longest Decade', about the last ten years of strife. Rose Neill joins as an announcer. Local production now averaging 10 hours per week.	Life of IBA extended to 1981. IBA extends ITV contracts to end 1981. IBA engineers demonstrate world's first digital videotape recorder. Significant network programme: 'South Bank Show' (LWT).
1979	Hour-long 'Good Evening Ulster', ground-breaking teatime magazine with Gloria Hunniford. Brum Henderson made a Fellow of the Royal Television Society. Brian Waddell becomes Controller of local programmes and a board member. 'Look and See', about educational resources in Northern Ireland. 'Build Your Own Boat' programme. Brougher Mtn UHF transmitter opened to serve Fermanagh area.	IBA given responsibility for fourth channel. ITV/ACTT dispute leads to eleven-week stoppage, losing over £90m in ad revenue. Significant network programme: 'Tiswas' (ATV/Central).
1980	Londonderry studio opened. Live show televised from the Grand Opera House to celebrate UTV's twenty-first anniversary. A new ident featuring a model of the station logo embedded on four faces of a cube coated in silver reclaimed through UTV film processing (silver nitrate on film emulsion). The ident first appears on 31 October 1980, and is used until September 1988.	IBA reappoints most ITV contracts. Southern TV and Westward TV are replaced by TVS and TSW. Associated TV restructured and based in east and west Midlands, becomes Central Independent. TV Broadcasting Act 1980 extends life of IBA to 1996 and expands its duties to include a fourth channel. Significant network programme: 'Death of a Princess' (ATV).
1981	Gloria Hunniford departs for BBC Radio 2 in London, leaving 'Good Evening Ulster'. Gary Gillespie and Gerry Kelly given a trial as presenters and the programme begins at 5.30 p.m. instead of 6 p.m.	UTV contract renewed. BCC (Broadcasting Complaints Commission) established. BARB (British Audience Research Bureau) created. Biggest outside broadcast ever: Charles and Diana's wedding. Five companies authorised to provide satellite TV services. First subscription TV service begins: Starview. Lord Thomson becomes chairman of the IBA. Significant network programme: 'Brideshead Revisited' (Granada).
1982	UTV crews go to Spain for the soccer World Cup. Northern Ireland wins group 5, eliminating Yugoslavia and beating Spain 1-0 on its home ground. Eamonn Holmes now presents 'Good Evening Ulster'. Outside broadcast unit used for the Assembly elections.	Channel 4 for England, Scotland and NI launched. S4C is the Welsh-language version for Wales. ITV franchise changes: ATV, Southern and Westward disappear. Replaced by Central, TVS and TSW. Sir Jeremy Isaacs is C4's first chief executive.

YEAR	UTV & UTV RELATED HISTORY	TV & CONTEXT HISTORY
		Launch of Satellite Television, later Sky Channel (Europe's first satellite channel). Significant network programme: 'Brookside' (Channel 4).
1983	'Irish RM' series – UTV co-production with RTÉ: three series to last to 1985. 'Ulster Landscapes', an eleven-part series by UTV and the new Channel 4. Outside Broadcast used in General Election. 'Trauma', 3-part series about the Royal Victoria Hospital, filmed over four months. Brum Henderson, MD and Deputy Chairman, becomes Chairman. Move from film to video tape for day-to-day operations. 'TV Play'. 'Hidden Curriculum' by Graham Reid. Video link between Havelock House and the UTV studio in Londonderry established. Desmond Smyth takes over as Managing Director. John McCann joins from the NI inward investment organisation as Financial Controller.	Start of breakfast television on the ITV network by TVAM in competition with BBC Breakfast Time. Significant network programme: 'Auf Wiedersehen Pet' (Central).
1984		Cable and Broadcasting Act and the Telecommunications Act. Swindon Cable the first cable service licensed. Significant network programme: 'Jewel in the Crown' (Granada).
1985	Eamonn Holmes leaves for BBC TV in Manchester. 'The Lesson is Ulster' – six-part documentary series about Ulster life, examining reasons behind the bigotry and violence. Senior UTV management granted share options in the company. Staff already benefit from a profit-sharing scheme.	As the Peacock Committee begins examining, among other issues, the case for advertising on the BBC, UTV comes out strongly against the idea. Closure of last 405-line transmitter. Cable Authority established, advertises first five franchises – Aberdeen cable is the first to start operations. Jon Davey first Director General.
1986	Peacock Committee advocates auctioning ITV programme contracts to the highest bidder, which UTV comes out against. (It eventually happened). UTV now producing 400 hours of local programmes, 100 more than the IBA contract requires.	Launch of NICAM digital stereo sound on television. IBA awards DBS (digital broadcast satellite) contract to BSB (British Satellite Broadcasting) for a three-channel service. Peacock proposes ITV franchise auctions.
1987	Two week strike at Easter, with UTV management running the station. For the launch of the station's new evening magazine programme, 'Six Tonight', in September 1987, a new ident is used, featuring a computer-animated silver station logo on a blue/green backdrop. This ident is UTV's first attempt at a CGI (Computer-Generated Imagery) ident. Community Service Announcements begun.	ITV contracts extended to 1992. IBA announce that 25 per cent of ITV programmes must be produced by independents (outside programme contractors). BBC agree the same. Broadcasting hours extended: Thames TV first to broadcast twenty-four hours. Advertising minutage limits extended from 7 to $7^1/_2$ minutes an hour. Significant network programme: 'Inspector Morse' (Central/Zenith). Industrial trouble takes normal programming off TV-am.
1988	Team briefing introduced to improve internal communication. UTV buys 50 per cent interest in local TV commercial and corporate video company HETV. Brian Waddell leaves to set up his own TV production company. Moore Sinnerton the new programme head. UTV supplies 24 hour broadcasting from network.	Astra satellites launched to carry television. White Paper recommends replacing IBA with ITC (Independent Television Commission). All ITV companies are now providing a 24-hour service.
1989	'Kelly' programme begins and will run for a remarkable seventeen years. Half million pound investment in SES, operator of the Astra TV satellites, pays off, as the company goes into profit. Takes 15 per cent stake in City Beat radio.	Sky Television launches four-channel service using the Astra satellite. IBA relaxes rules on sponsorship (of weather forecasts, arts and instructional programmes) and on advertising by charities.

YEAR	UTV & UTV RELATED HISTORY	TV & CONTEXT HISTORY
1990	Brum Henderson resigns as Chairman acrimoniously after over thirty years' association with the company. JB McGuckian, vice-chairman, takes over. Maurice Smyth new programme head. Lord Mayor of Belfast, Reg Empey, visits Havelock House and Telethon 90, which raises £600,000 for local charities.	
1991	UTV retains the Northern Ireland TV franchise with a cash bid of £1.027 million per annum. £3 million expansion of Havelock House, including provision of new 2,500 sq. ft studio. TSMS (Television Sales and Marketing Services) appointed to sell UTV's national airtime. Highest share of viewing throughout the year, at times 40 per cent greater than nearest rival, BBC NI.	IBA becomes the ITC. TV listings deregulated. ITC awards licenses (one national and fifteen regional). Significant network programmes: 'Prime Suspect' (Granada); 'GBH' (C4). Broadcasting Act 1990 allowing auction of ITV franchises and auction of a Channel 5.
1992	John McCann, General Manager, appointed to the board. Alan Bremner new programme head. 25 per cent independent production now a statutory requirement. UTV also loses selling Channel 4 advertising – now sells its own. UTV says UK economy slowly emerging from recession. 20 per cent of advertising now from Dublin, and TSMS opens a Dublin office to sell UTV airtime. NI also providing 20 per cent of advertising. The rest from Gt Britain.	ITV network centre created, Marcus Plantin its first director. ITC advertise C5 licence, only one application. ITC draw up and award C4 licence. ITC announce networking system: OFT to consult on fairness. Significant network programme: 'Big Breakfast' (C4).
1993	'Faces of Ulster' series, featuring Jack McCann, Neil Shawcross, John Campbell, Vincent Campbell, Rowel Friers. At 6 p.m. on 4 June 1993, UTV officially unveils a new UTV logo. Announcements and trailers refer to UTV and not 'Ulster Television', and the station's news service re-branded as 'UTV Live'. Oracle outbid and replaced by Teletext Ltd.	ITC mounts first public demonstration of digital terrestrial TV. Government relaxes rules on ITV takeovers. Yorkshire buys Tyne Tees and becomes YT-T. New ITV licenses: Carlton, Meridian, Westcountry, GMTV replace Thames, TVS, TSW and TV-am. Significant network programme: 'Cracker' (Granada).
1994	Two ceasefires announced. UTV falls foul of TV-am and the ITC for breaking into TV-am airtime without authority to announce the IRA ceasefire. 'Counterpoint', award-winning programme on paedophile priest, rocks the Catholic Church and Irish establishment.	Carlton takes over Central, Granada takes over LWT, MAI takes over Anglia. White Paper: BSC and BCC to merge. ABC's 'World News Now' broadcast over the internet.
1995	UTV provides 600 hrs of local programming, 100 more than contractually required. Two dozen independent producers commissioned. Twenty-five cameras deployed for visit of President Clinton. 'Kelly' programme visits Chernobyl. 'Lesser Spotted Ulster' from Joe Mahon begins.	Channel 5 licence auction: Channel 5 Broadcasting wins (Pearson and MAI). New cross-media ownership rules announced. Cable reaches 1 million subscribers.
1996	120 channels now available in NI, but UTV averages a 42 per cent share of viewing and some 50 per cent more viewers than BBC NI. In the 6 p.m.–7 p.m. slot, 'UTV Live at Six' has 49 per cent, a twenty-point lead over BBC NI's 'Newsline'. Schedule changed to accommodate Canary Wharf bomb, which ends first IRA ceasefire. Round-the-clock coverage of Drumcree standoff during the Twelfth. The ITC reports that UTV has 'maintained and in some cases improved' the quality of 'well resourced' regional programmes. The long-running 'Counterpoint' is honoured with third International Celtic Film and Television Festival award for current affairs programming. 122 schools take part in the School Choir of the Year competition.	United Newspapers and MAI merge (United News and Media). OFT investigates sporting rights. First pay-per-view event: Sky charge for Bruno v Tyson. Broadcasting Act: media ownership, digital TV, BSC & BCC to merge. Carlton Communications buys Westcountry. Judicial review over ITC's awarding of C5 licence finds in favour of ITC.

YEAR	UTV & UTV RELATED HISTORY	TV & CONTEXT HISTORY
1997	UTV maintains position as most viewed channel in the UK, with peak-time share of 43 per cent, against 38 per cent for the ITV network. 'Ultimate Ulster' begins, based on survey of top entertainment and leisure venues in NI. 'Counterpoint' name dropped in favour of 'UTV Live Insight'. 170 schools in School Choir of the Year competition.	Sir Robin Biggam becomes chairman of the ITC. United News and Media takes over HTV. Scottish Media takes over Grampian TV. Granada takes over Yorkshire Tyne-Tees TV. BDB wins three digital multiplex licences. Digital 3 & 4 and SDN awarded the other two digital multiplex licences. Channel 4 funding formula payments to be phased out. C5 launched. Michael Grade resigns from Channel 4, succeeded by Michael Jackson. Significant network programme: funeral of Princess of Wales, watched by 31 million.
1998	Coverage of Good Friday Agreement and the Omagh bomb, known as the worst single atrocity of the Troubles. 'Insight' wins BT Institute of Public Relations award for best TV current affairs programme. Omagh programme nominated by ITV for a Grierson Trust award, awarded annually to the best documentary film-making from Britain and abroad.	ITC alters the terms for renewing ITV license. BSkyB and BDB row over set-top boxes. Sky Digital launched. Digital terrestrial transmission launches as BDB becomes ONdigital. Introduction of digital widescreen. ITC allow ITV to move 'News at Ten'. ITV2 launched as a 24 hour free-to-air entertainment television digital channel. Westcountry renamed Carlton Westcountry. Significant network programme: 'Who Wants To Be A Millionaire?' (Celador).
1999	John McCann appointed Managing Director on the retirement of Desmond Smyth. UTV enters the internet business by buying Direct Net Access (DNA). ITV early evening news moved to 6.30 p.m. so 'UTV Live at Six' reduced to 30 minutes. 'UTV Life', new programme, introduced at 5.30 p.m. 'Coronation Street' interrupted for the first time for live coverage of Stormont talks. Coverage of power-sharing executive formation. UTV2 launched in 1999 as TV You on Digital Terrestrial Television in Northern Ireland, simulcasting ITV2 in England, Wales and the Scottish Borders. Unusually, neither UTV2 nor its predecessor carry any advertising, since the station is only receivable by a few thousand viewers.	Ntl launches digital cable TV. BSkyB hits 1m subscribers. Free set-top boxes to encourage digital take-up. Granada buys 9.9 per cent of LFC (starts frenzy of TV companies buying into football). 'News at Ten' ends. Government announces probable end date for analogue TV. (2012 for Northern Ireland).
2000	UTV Internet launched. Bumper year, with operating profit up 30 per cent to £14 million. £13 million from sale of SES satellite shares. First steps into acquiring radio stations in Ireland. Jim Downey, financial controller, appointed to board. UTV along with main TV channels, switches from the old 4:3 aspect screen to a new widescreen 14:9 on analogue transmissions and 16:9 for digital. To mark the occasion, UTV introduce a new set of idents using footage from the 1996 landscape idents. These UTV idents the first in 16:9 aspect ratio. Granada Media take over TSMS and its sale of UTV airtime.	Carlton and United announce merger plans. Granada buys Meridian, Anglia and HTV. Carlton buys HTV. ITC force 'News at Ten' to go back to ten o'clock after ratings drop. Annual sales of widescreen TVs exceeds one million. Capital Radio Group buys Border TV. Media Holdings Group buys Channel TV. BSkyB reaches 5 million subscribers. White paper plans for Ofcom (replacing the ITC) announced. Significant network programme: 'Big Brother' (C4).
2001	The 1993 logo is replaced with a similar but flatter and wider logo. The 'U' is rendered in yellow on a blue oblong, with the 'TV' in red on a yellow oblong contained inside the blue oblong. Its first use is in UTV's Christmas ident in 2000, and in January 2001, a new series of idents is launched, shot at various locations across Northern Ireland, including the Silent Valley Reservoir in County Down, Great Victoria Street in Belfast and the Hands Across the Divide sculpture at the Craigavon Bridge, Derry.	ITV finally agree deal to be carried on Sky Digital. ONdigital reaches 1 million subscribers. United sell off shares in C5 – completing their withdrawal from British TV. ITC cut licence payments to aid digital switch. Sky turns off its analogue service. Michael Jackson quits C4: succeeded by Mark Thompson.

YEAR	UTV & UTV RELATED HISTORY	TV & CONTEXT HISTORY
2002	Worst communal violence for twenty years. Stormont suspended. UTV has almost 50 per cent more peak-time viewers than all the satellite and Republic of Ireland channels combined (240 channels in total). Furthermore UTV's peak-time audience equals the combined shares of all the other commercial channels – every satellite channel plus all four Irish channels, Channel 4 and Channel 5. UTV opts out of a common look with the ITV1 brand, replacing individual station logos. UTV2 closes on 22 January 2002.	ONdigital goes into administration. Freeview begins. Pace launch a £100 set-top box, giving access to a basic package of free digital channels. ITV Digital goes into administration, unable to fulfil its contract with the Football League, and is put up for sale. Lord Currie of Marylebone is appointed chair of Ofcom.
2003	New media three-fold increase in operating profit. Irish radio stations are a quasi-national advertising outlet. Internet revenues up 80 per cent. Net TV advertising up 2.1 per cent, in contrast to ITV's 3.4 per cent decline.	Regulation of independent TV passes to Ofcom, superseding ITC and other regulatory bodies.
2004	UTV increases its peak-time share as well as its lead over the ITV network's average, even though almost 60 per cent of homes in Northern Ireland have over 250 TV channels. Almost all programmes subtitled. New computer system for newsroom. Switch to server-based transmission systems, moving from tape-based commercial transmission to disk drive servers. Station idents and programme trails also move to transmission off hard drives, as do some filmed news inserts. UTV telephony introduced throughout Ireland.	Merger of Granada and Carlton. Merged company is called ITV plc. BBC Chairman of Governors and Director General both resign in wake of Hutton Report.
2005	U105, UTV's radio station aimed at the over 45s in the Belfast area, begins. UTV the third most watched channel in 80 per cent of multi-channel Republic of Ireland homes. UTV's investigative current affairs programme 'Insight' wins Royal Television Society (RTS) Nations and Regions Current Affairs Award for the second year running. One-hour obituary programme for George Best. Acquisition of Wireless Group, which owns the TalkSport station. 'Kelly' programme comes to an end after seventeen years.	ITV celebrates its half-century. Ofcom publishes Phase 3 of a Report into Public Service Broadcasting.
2006	Alan Bremner retires as programme head. Michael Wilson appointed MD of television. 'UTV Live at Six' the UK's most watched regional news programme, averaging 168,000 viewers. Company name changed from Ulster Television plc to UTV plc. The existing name no longer reflects the full scope of the company's business.	BBC, ITV, Channel 4 and Five start HD terrestrial trial using MPEG4 coding from Crystal Palace transmitter. Not available for general viewing. First event covered is football World Cup. ITV begins HD trials on cable.
2007	'Lesser Spotted Ulster' and 'Ultimate Ulster' rated best-performing regional programmes in the whole ITV network. New UTV idents on screen, featuring newly recorded landscape scenes from across Northern Ireland. The new idents are used initially to promote the 'Ultimate Ulster' series. Corporate reorganisation, in which UTV shareholders exchange their shares for shares in a new holding company, UTV Media plc, which took over UTV plc's shareholdings in the new media and radio subsidiaries. UTV plc – the original Ulster Television Limited, now a wholly owned subsidiary of UTV Media – has returned to being solely the operating company for the ITV franchise.	First analogue switch-off: BBC2 signal at Whitehaven, Cumbria. 'Coronation Street' remains Northern Ireland's favourite programme with a 61 per cent share of audience, followed closely by another ITV soap, 'Emmerdale'.
2008	Tibus web company in Belfast purchased.	As its financial health fails, ITV plc claims increased fee for network from UTV, Scottish and Channel television (who are not part of ITV plc). The three stations reject the claim.
2009	UTV achieves its half-century.	

1959–2009

Chapter 1

A very early picture of Anne Gregg taken for publicity purposes outside Havelock House. Anne, along with Ivor Mills, had been a civil servant and became an original presenter for the 'Roundabout' programme. Beside Anne is Paddy Scott, who was UTV's first producer.

The
beginnings

I t was touch and go as to whether Britain was to have an independent television system. It probably would have happened eventually, but not necessarily as soon as 1955.

In 1951, an election in the UK overturned the Labour government elected just after World War II. In came a Conservative government headed once again by the wartime leader Winston Churchill, a rebuke to ageism since he was now 77. He might have been an old man, but he was not set in his ways. The BBC charter was up for renewal, which presented an opportunity to reform broadcasting. Most of the Cabinet was unadventurous by inclination and it was thought that the BBC would retain a monopoly. Churchill himself was known to be dismissive of the idea of commercial television. However, some of his own backbenchers began to change attitudes, responding to pressure from both the population and the manufacturers of television sets.

The pro-commercial television lobby was able to build upon a feeling many Conservatives had that the BBC had been biased against them during their spell of opposition (a recurring refrain from UK governments of both left and right – then and now). The success of Radio Luxembourg influenced the debate. It broadcast over Britain and Ireland from the continental mainland on 208-metres medium wave, and was commercial and populist. In the fifties it restricted its English-language programmes to the evenings and proved to be an effective advertising platform. I listened myself as a child and can still recall the sponsored time checks, the 'H. Samuel Everite watch time'.

In the end, the tide of opinion within government turned against the BBC monopoly and in favour of competition within broadcasting. In 1953 the Government published a document outlining a policy for television and this led, after heated debate, to the Television Act of 1954, which at last gave commercial television the green light. The word 'commercial' was sidelined in favour of the word 'independent' (meaning independent of the BBC) and sponsorship was forbidden for fear of programme content being interfered with. Advertisers could simply buy airtime spots in much the same way they could buy space on the page of a newspaper or magazine.

The test transmission card which appeared on the 405-line YHF service prior to UTV coming on air in 1959.

To oversee the new television, the Act created the Independent Television Authority (ITA) under the chairmanship of Sir Kenneth Clark, later Lord Clark, with a remit of ten years. It might have been thought that an eminent art historian, a former director of the National Gallery in London and former Surveyor of the King's Pictures responsible for the art collections in Buckingham Palace, Windsor Castle, and other royal establishments was not an obvious choice for heading an ITA charged with setting up a populist commercial channel. But Kenneth Clark loved the medium and the medium loved him. He was so good in front of camera that when he left in 1954, the legendary Lew Grade, as managing director of ATV (one of the new ITV companies), offered him a contract as a television presenter. The result was that on 19 November 1959, only twenty days after UTV began transmitting, Kenneth Clark presented Ulster viewers with a programme on the painter Goya. Clark's genius lay in his appreciation that television was, and always would be, a performer's medium, no matter what the subject.

Kenneth Clark's ITA came up with a regional federal structure for ITV. There were to be a number of companies, such as UTV, appointed by the Authority up and down the country, and together they would co-operate to produce programmes for the schedule.

From the beginning, the independent or commercial television system was plural and regional. The first Television Act of 1954 required the Authority to do all it could to ensure adequate competition to supply programmes among a number of separate programme companies. The Act also stipulated that every individual TV station should have a 'suitable proportion of matter calculated to appeal specially to the tastes and outlook of persons served by the station or stations'. In the case of Northern Ireland, therefore, a station serving the province was required to be populist to some degree, though it might have been thought that since the success of advertising required maximisation of viewership, such a requirement was hardly needed in any area. If a station did not appeal to its region, it would fail.

The ITA knew that television production would be costly. Large resources in finance and technical equipment, and a skilled specialised workforce, would be needed for regular weekly light entertainment, drama and current affairs productions. The BBC managed this by having a central base in London which produced the overwhelming majority of programmes for its network. This solution would not be open to a federation of regional television companies, so another device to provide a network was needed. The ITA therefore thrust the task of producing the backbone network mainly upon the largest companies, which could expect a higher revenue from the areas they served. It created a system made up of two types of TV station. There were to be several large so-called network companies, complemented by a number of smaller regional companies, of which Ulster Television would be one of the smallest.

While they made some programmes for audiences in their own area, the network companies also made programmes for the whole country, programmes like 'Coronation Street' and other dramas, national news (from ITN) and current affairs, major entertainment and so forth. The first task of the smaller regional companies was held to be production for their own areas. From 1955–68 there were four major or network companies; there have been five since 1968, providing a central core of programmes for the whole country, that is, both for themselves and for the ten regional companies. In recent times all the licences for commercial television in England and Wales have come under the ownership of ITV plc, something which could not have happened under the original structure. Only Ulster Television, Scottish Television and the diminutive Channel Island stations survive as separate entities from this era.

The five largest companies – Thames, London Weekend, ATV, Granada and Yorkshire – were from 1968 the main providers of network programmes to be used by the whole service. Therefore, areas served by these network companies were planned to be large enough to give them the income needed to carry out this task. Two were based in London, and the other three in Manchester, Leeds and Birmingham.

The primary reason for the existence of the smaller regional companies like Ulster Television was for the provision of truly local programme services. These local companies, although minnows compared with the big five, could also occasionally contribute programmes to the network. Local programme initiatives led to the adoption of programme ideas by other companies, and contributions to the development of news magazines, adult education, school and religious programmes have stemmed from the regional companies. Arrangements existed for the regular scrutiny of available programmes from the regions with a view to a network showing. During the Troubles in Northern Ireland, for example, Ulster Television pictures were frequently networked as part of national news programmes, although it tended to exasperate the company that it was so difficult to persuade the network to take anything other than Troubles-related material.

On Thursday 22 September 1955, the first ITV company, Associated-Rediffusion, contracted by the ITA to supply programmes to greater London on weekdays, began at 7.15 p.m., broadcasting the national and international news supplied to it from the studios of ITN. The first advertisement was for Gibbs SR toothpaste and was followed by others, including ads for Cadbury's chocolate and

OFF-AIR

No. 4   THE HOUSE MAGAZINE OF ULSTER TELEVISION   AUTUMN 1985

Keep up the good work

For the first few editions of our house magazine we were beginning to think that nothing ever happened to anyone in the place. They didn't seem to go anywhere, or do anything.

That's the way it seemed. Or everyone was too shy to tell us about it.

This time, however, we have a much bigger selection of items and the bits and pieces of information have been rolling in quite nicely, thank you. So keep it up.

It is YOUR magazine and the editorial committee will only be too pleased to help with the spelling, or putting in the big letters where you have stupidly (sorry, inadvertently) put in a little one.

With this edition we are celebrating another ULSTER TELEVISION birthday on October 31 — the company's 26th.

And on the back page there are lots of pictures of the second anniversary buffet and disco of the Sports and Social Club held in the Wellington Park Hotel on October 8.

There's a report, too, on the Sports and Social Club's activities, an update on "that clubhouse", and attractive travel offers.

The golfers, fishermen, the hockey team and the runners are all well represented this time in the sports section.

And Alan McMurtry serves up a large "dishful" of the latest information on satellite television reception, as well as a nostalgic look back at its earliest days with a crystal set.

Ramsey Nelson and Paul Irwin suitably kitted out for another of their sorties for ABOUT BRITAIN.

Things that can happen on location

You might think that David Scott and Jim McGirr (below) are a bit old to be playing with toy trains, but they were certainly on the right track while filming Andy Crockart's MODEL MAGIC series, which has been going out on Channel Four.

They had smoke in their eyes and mud on their boots for five weeks of filming which included locations in London and the south of England.

—•—

Sound recordist Peter Gregory has been known to utter the odd derogatory remark about Blane Scott's driving.

But he thought he was safe enough while filming at Funderland when the intrepid duo stepped into a dodgem for some action footage.

Unfortunately Blane accidentally hit the accelerator as Peter was half-way in, and off they shot across the track with Peter frantically balancing the recorder, cable and mic while trying to climb in.

—•—

Jeanie Johnston and the crew were very impressed with the lay-out of the City Hospital's new tower block, in spite of all that's been said about it.

"It only takes 30 seconds to go from top to bottom in these high speed lifts", enthused our guide.

"They're computerised and — (embarrassed pause) — that's probably why we've just got jammed between floors!"

—•—

Have you heard the one about the spark who went to do a story on computers?

He pulled out a few plugs to make room for his lights, carefully re-connecting them all into his adaptor. Then the boffin switched on his computer to find all his carefully prepared programmes — Wiped.

I won't tell you his name, but Al bet you can guess.

—•—

In Fermanagh, Blane Scott's crew spent an enlightening day with the Hare Krishna community on their island. Lunch was slightly different than in the UTV canteen — pudding and main course all came on one plate and was eaten cross legged on the floor. (We won't mention who had holes in their socks). But the main source of amazement was the vegetarian cat who lived there — just what does it do when it meets a mouse on the stairs, say "Go in peace, brother!" J.J.

Smoke gets in your lens . . . David Scott and Jim McGirr playing trains at the Transport Museum while shooting MODEL MAGIC.

Even meals on wheels

JOHN GAFFIKIN COWAN brings you up-to-date on the Sports and Social Club

The Sports and Social Club celebrated its Birthday on Tuesday, October 8, in the Wellington Park Hotel amid the usual jollification for which the Club has become notorious.

Members and their guests were treated to a magnificent buffet supper and then proceeded to dance the excess weight off to the sound of the Welly disco.

For the less energetic the bar continued to serve beverages until the early hours of the morning.

During the course of the evening a draw was held to distribute meals for two at most of the major hotels in town, and various large bottles which had been kindly donated to the Club. Even the members back at base were not forgotten, as Jackie Corbett gallantly organised a meals-on-wheels service to Havelock House. All present agreed that the evening was a fitting celebration for the Club's anniversary.

OUTLAY

Although the Committee is still actively pursuing every avenue to provide an actual Club House, it was with regret that the decision was made not to continue with the "Brown's" project.

After having investigated the financial side of the proposal the Committee realised that the outlay — rent, rates, insurance, refurbishing and security — would not justify what would after all only be a short-term solution to the Club House problem.

On consideration it was felt wiser to wait for a property or site which could become a permanent home for the Club.

CHEAP TRIPS

For the second year running, the Club has decided to offer to members the facility for London shopping trips.

This year the offer of half-price travel to London (for members only) has been extended to include sea travel, so that members may take their cars to the "mainland", and it will apply for the whole month of November.

Interested members should book through Roberta McMahon.

Although it is over seven weeks until Christmas, the dynamic Committee are hard at work organising a Christmas Party. Like the successful event last year, this will take the form of a Dinner Dance.

Rumours to the effect that the top room of Maxi's has been booked are totally false, though the N.U.J. may well be having one of their celebrations there.

The SSC's party will be at one of the more conventional establishments, after a seasonal meal it is planned to have dancing to a live band, perhaps one not totally unconnected with the company.

When the final details of time, date (probably the week before Christmas) and venue, have been finalised they will be loudly announced on the SSC Notice Board.

For those who have still not found this elusive Board, it is directly opposite the lift, at the side of the door into Studio One. (See also News in Brief on Page 2).

Norman Rees, of ITN, with Colm McWilliams and Derek Murray at the welcoming dinner for the news editors.

Editors' visit

A party of almost 30 News Editors from ITN and the Network companies were the guests of Ulster Television when they were here for one of their regular conferences on October 25.

Managing Director, Desmond Smyth hosted a reception for the visitors at Havelock House and a dinner at the Conway Hotel on the evening before the event.

These get-togethers are held a couple of times a year around the different regions, but this was the first time that the Editors had been here since 1968, just before the start of the troubles.

As usual there was a valuable exchange of information and ideas to keep the news flowing smoothly between the various Network companies and Wells Street, and also to iron out any problems about exchanging topical items between the regions themselves.

Our Miss is missing

The response to our competition to find a "Miss Off-Air" seems to have Miss-fired a bit. There were a couple of recognisable names. But when Forensic put the bits of paper together it was obviously one person who couldn't make up their mind.

Another entry, complete with revealing colour picture and a list of "sponsors" had to be regrettably rejected, as we might risk prosecution under the Obscene Publications Act, threats from Greenpeace and action by Maxies, who hold the copyright of his original portrait.

What the four-inch nail was doing in the entry folder still mystifies us.

We will maybe have another crack at picking a Personality Girl next time.

Holiday snaps

We did have a few entries for the Holiday Snaps competition. Some were very good, but the very moody scenes, with sunset and clouds were just a little dark for reproduction from colour to black and white.

But we will keep them in hand, and hope that more entries will come in so that we can show a selection of them in the next issue.

Esso petrol. Two days later, ATV (Associated Television), contracted for the weekends, began. The system worked rather well right from the start. A leader in the first issue of the original ITV programme listings paper, the *TV Times*, published in 1955, read:

> So far television in this country has been a monopoly restricted by limited finance and often, or so it seemed, restricted by a lofty attitude towards the wishes of viewers by those in control. That situation has now undergone a great and dramatic change. Viewers will no longer have to accept what has been deemed best for them. They will be able to pick and choose. And the new Independent Television programme planners aim at giving viewers what viewers want – at the time viewers want it.

The *TV Times* could be expected to write in support of the new populist network, since that was the function of the paper. The first edition featured a picture of Lucille Ball, whose domestic comedy show, 'I Love Lucy', aired at the peak time of nine o'clock on a Sunday evening. The BBC had not been programming like that. It would never have had shows like Hughie Green's 'Double your Money', or Michael Miles's 'Take your Pick', both with cash prizes. And there was 'Sunday Night at the London Palladium' with its host, Tommy Trinder. All programmes aimed at a mass audience and shown at a time when a mass audience wanted to view them.

Around half of television sets were bought on credit terms. For some reason, the Government decided to try and discourage the public from purchasing such expensive items by forcing the initial payment to be at least a third of the total cost and requiring the balance to be paid within eighteen months. This could not have come at a worse time for television sales in Scotland, a month before the opening of Scotland's first TV transmitter at Kirk o'Shotts. The Scots felt doubly aggrieved because, largely thanks to tax increases, the cheapest TV set was now some 60 per cent more expensive than when the more affluent south of England had bought their sets.

Then it was Northern Ireland's turn to have an independent station. Enter Sydney Box, a noted film producer and screenwriter. One of his later films was a well-regarded spoof spy thriller, *Deadlier than the Male*, featuring detective Bulldog

Drummond, who is matched against a an evil megalomaniac with a bunch of female assassins at his beck and call. Sydney produced almost forty films and scripted twenty-six. Two details link him with Ulster Television. He was on the board of Tyne Tees Television, which had gone through the selection process ahead of Ulster. Secondly, he was a friend and colleague of another noted film producer, Bill MacQuitty. Bill, or William MacQuitty, to give him his screen credit name, was the producer of *A Night to Remember*. Bill MacQuitty was quite an extraordinary figure and UTV owes its existence to him. Sydney Box urged Bill to do exactly as he had done, to involve himself in this new business of television and go for the Northern Ireland franchise that the Independent Television Authority planned to introduce at the end of 1958.

Bill MacQuitty in his home near the end of his life. He was UTV's first managing director and chose 29-year-old Brum Henderson to be his successor.

Bill MacQuitty was born in Northern Ireland, the son of the managing director of the *Belfast Telegraph*, and educated at Campbell College. Determined to escape the narrow world of Northern Ireland, he applied, at the age of eighteen, to the Chartered Bank of India, Australia and China, and headed off. He was twenty-one when he took up his first posting in Amritsar in Punjab. The bank evidently had little idea about the young man they had employed. In l932, the bank's company secretary was disturbed by reports that MacQuitty had learnt Urdu, taken up yoga, become a Buddhist and scandalously broken the colour bar, strictly adhered to by the white raj. 'I wonder if you don't have too much interest in life to make

SPRING
FEATURE
FILMS

ULSTER TELEVISION

There is little doubt that television affected cinema audiences. In the sixties and beyond, UTV boasted about the films it was showing. All these film-star faces would have been familiar in the sixties. How many can be named now?

a good banker?' he asked MacQuitty. Eventually Bill left banking to begin farming in Northern Ireland and in his spare time made a film about silage. This caught the attention of the Ministry of Information and thus was launched his career in film-making, during World War II. MacQuitty began working with Sydney Box, already an established and prolific film documentary-maker. From there he moved into feature films. He had never forgotten as a six-year-old witnessing the launch of the *Titanic* in Belfast, an experience which led eventually to his film, *A Night to Remember*. MacQuitty was tremendously pleased when James Cameron, writer and director of the 1997 film *Titanic*, starring Leonardo DiCaprio and Kate Winslet, thanked him for his vision in creating *A Night to Remember*. Cameron told him that it had caused 'a ripple effect through modern culture', which had partly inspired his own film. If that is so, then Bill is a forgotten hero, whose statue ought to be somewhere in Belfast's emerging *Titanic* quarter. There would be plenty to put on the plaque pertaining to this Renaissance man. His first book was about the temple of Abu Simbel, whose cause he fought as the waters trapped behind the Aswan High Dam were rising to engulf it.

His obituary in the London *Times* in 1998 said:

> He went on to produce almost a book a year on a variety of subjects, reflecting his interests in the Orient, all illustrated with his award-winning photographs from a library of a quarter of a million taken by him over 60 years in 75 different countries. *Buddha*, published in 1969, included a foreword by the Dalai Lama, and in 1971 the Shah of Iran sponsored a large volume to commemorate the 2,500th anniversary of his country. MacQuitty's gardening expertise was highlighted in two books, *Irish Gardens* and *Great Botanical Gardens of the World*. His most successful book was *Tutankhamun: The Last Journey*, which sold half a million copies. His evocative photograph of Tutankhamun's funerary mask was seen all over the world, as it was used as the poster for the 1972 British Museum exhibition of the tomb's treasures.

This was the man Sydney Box asked to start an independent television station in Northern Ireland. The idea did not immediately attract Bill, but his brother James liked the idea and began to work on it, with the help of Bill and Sydney. Others had thought about the same idea, including the *Belfast Telegraph*, where the brothers' father had been managing director, and the *News Letter*. However, few people in either newspaper were optimistic that the project would be viable. Many others thought the same and for good reason. As MacQuitty himself wrote in his autobiography, *A Life to Remember*:

> My brother met with scant enthusiasm for his proposals, and grounds for doubt certainly existed. At that stage, the BBC was producing only a few minutes of broadcasting time a day for the region. In theory, a million people would be able to receive the new channel, but the [TV] set count so far stood at only 80,000. This would yield an annual income from advertising of about £400,000, out of which the winning contractor would have to pay a licence fee of £100,000, produce seven hours a week of local programmes and buy in enough product to fill the rest of the air time with material as good as that of the big stations whose incomes ran to many millions. It was also going to be necessary to build and equip expensive hi-tech studios, recruit highly skilled, highly paid and heavily unionized staff and maintain harmonious relations with a dangerously divided community. Small wonder if the response to my brother's appeal evoked a thunderous silence.

The only people who thought there was mileage in the idea were already in a group, headed by one of the province's other daily newspapers, the *Northern Whig*, and its managing director, Lieutenant-Colonel Cunningham.

As it happened, Bill needed to talk to George Lodge, owner and manager of the Royal Hippodrome cinema in Belfast (and who had shown his film on silage), about a premiere for *A Night to Remember*. Lodge was in the Cunningham group and thought Bill, with his film experience, would be a good extra member of the team. But the Cunninghams of the *Whig* did not think so. They had already asked an American TV company for its expertise and obviously thought Bill would not fit with that idea. It is interesting to speculate that if they had brought Bill MacQuitty into their consortium, the history of ITV in Northern Ireland could have been very different.

Some years previously, when Bill was still farming, he would often go to the Crawfordsburn Inn in the middle of Crawfordsburn village, close to the North

Down coast, for pig swill. Feeding kitchen leftovers to pigs was common farming practice until banned after the 2001 outbreak of foot-and-mouth disease. The owner of the Crawfordsburn Inn was a man called Paddy Falloon, whom Bill had got to know. Bill now went to see Falloon, brandishing a copy of the Tyne Tees license application, a present from Sydney Box. He showed it to Paddy and asked him for any contacts who might join in a similar venture for Northern Ireland.

As Bill MacQuitty recounted:

> The next day he took me to meet the Catherwoods, father and son, and Major George McKean, who had interests in transport and building work. They grilled me up and down, especially about any English shareholders who might gain control of the company. Eventually I suggested a shareholding of 51 per cent for Ulster, 25 per cent held in reserve for a local newspaper and, for the English investors, including myself, 24 per cent. On this basis, McKean said he would put in money, and the others followed suit. A steering committee was formed, with my brother in the chair, and Paddy suggested Lord Antrim for our group's chairman.
>
> The News Letter and Belfast Telegraph were invited to join and turned the proposal down, but Commander Oscar Henderson and his two sons, Captain Bill and Brumwell 'Brum' Henderson, part-owners of the News Letter came in, as did two of my Baird cousins who were part-owners of the Belfast Telegraph.
>
> It became obvious that it would help our application if we could back up our representative spread of influential Northern Ireland people with some entertainment talent from London. I therefore invited Sir Laurence Olivier, Betty Box, Bea Lillie (herself of Ulster stock) and Sir John Rothenstein, Director of the Tate Gallery, to join us, which they did. Sydney came over and he and Brum spent two days at Paddy's Inn at Crawfordsburn creating our application. The name we chose for our company was 'Ulster Television'. Our apt and unique logo, the track of a flying spot zigzagging across the screen, was the result of a competition.

It was designed by 21-year-old Roy Irwin of Ballycarry, Co. Antrim. His design was chosen from more than 450 entries. Roy completed his apprenticeship as a lithographic artist in the summer of 1959.

And that was the birth of Ulster Television. Except, of course, that the Cunningham competitors had to be defeated. The selection process by the ITA involved the submission of papers and an interview with consortium directors, which took place on the afternoon of Tuesday 4 November 1958 in the ITA office, Prince's Gate, Kensington, London, overlooking Hyde Park. The Cunningham application, headed by another peer of the realm, the Duke of Abercorn, had been interviewed on the morning of the same day. As luck would have it, both delegations were on the same plane over to London, the Ulster Television one consisting of Lord Antrim, William MacQuitty, Captain Bill Henderson and chartered accountant George Cameron. An interesting commentary upon the times is that the Ulster Television delegation noted that the other delegation had boarded the plane with a pair of shotguns. They wondered jocularly if the intention of the Duke of Abercorn delegation was to shoot the Lord Antrim delegation. In this very different age, the idea of attempting to board an aircraft carrying guns as hand luggage would be regarded as either insane or wicked.

The chairman of the ITA was by now Sir Ivone Kirkpatrick, a retired career diplomat. He was born in India of a Catholic Irish Limerick family and had left school to join the Royal Inniskilling Fusiliers and then the British diplomatic corps, serving in Italy and Germany in the years up to 1939. During World War II, he had been controller of the European Services of the BBC. Sir Ivone told the Ulster Television group that his committee liked their application, but observed that of the eighteen directors chosen to act as a balanced representation of Northern Ireland's divided society, only one had any experience of television and film. He was referring to MacQuitty himself, who quickly assured Sir Ivone that he had lined up experienced programme producers to employ. But Sir Ivone pushed further, with the direct question MacQuitty could not duck: 'Mr MacQuitty, would you be prepared to take time off from film production and put the company on air?'

MacQuitty had been fearing this question. Undoubtedly he had prepared for it, because he knew that the success or failure of his group hung upon his answer. Unpleasant images of what it is like to be a managing director flooded into his mind. As he put it, 'I could see myself, as managing director, beginning to drown before long in drafting lengthy reports on the merits of this or that system, and endeavouring to explain the rights of the numerous trade unions without whom no TV company can exist; not to say, yearning for the simplicity of my partnership with Sydney Box and our ability to make headway without ever holding a board meeting.' Everyone in that ITA room was looking at Bill, waiting, until he answered the crucial question with the words, 'I will.'

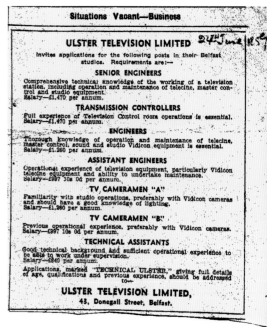

Engineering jobs advertised in June 1959. The new station put itself on air in under a year, which was quite an achievement.

They won. They then had less than a year to find premises, build studios, technical areas and offices and recruit technical, sales and programme teams. True to his word, Bill MacQuitty signed, reluctantly, a contract which ran for a year from 1 January 1959. When a new Speaker of the House of Commons is elected, the successful candidate is physically dragged to the chair by other MPs. It is an amiable charade which has its roots in the Speaker's historic function of communicating the Commons' opinions to the monarch, who might not want to hear them, in which case there could be unpleasant side effects for that Speaker. Hence prudent reluctance.

But Bill MacQuitty was not feigning reluctance whilst being dragged by circumstances to the top executive's chair. He really did hate any form of contract and future commitment, and this is very evident in the conditions of the contract. His first six months were to be full-time, the second six months half-time – on half pay. So, added to the list of company tasks for that first frantic year was finding a replacement managing director, a prospect which MacQuitty regarded as the most daunting.

Chapter 2

'It's All Happening' was one of the first late-night studio magazine programmes mounted by Ulster Television towards the end of the sixties. The show went out on Friday night and was a mix of news, controversial and provocative interviews, satire, poetry and jazz. Standing in the background is Ian Hill, the author and journalist. Sitting on the left is presenter David Mahlow. Myles Scott, with his hand raised, is the floor manager.

Early days

When the celebrations of winning the contest had died down, a frenzy of work began in an attempt to have the station, Ulster Television, ready for a target date of Hallowe'en 1959. Every day they were not on air was now a day of expenditure without income.

Putting the bid together had cost the directors just £1,000, but now they really had to spend fast. They needed some staff. For the time being, a little Ulster Television group camped in at 43 Donegall Street, a property a few yards from the *News Letter* owned by one of the bigger shareholders, Ivan Pollin. Brum Henderson by now had as a secretary Valerie Johnston, who had been invited to join by the chairman, Lord Antrim. Their finance man was another Johnston, Barry, who was known to both Brum and Lord Antrim. Gordon Duffield was another early employee and he remembers the serendipity of the recruitment process:

I was a journalist on the Belfast Telegraph and was also a correspondent for the cinema magazine, *Kine Weekly*. One day George Lodge of Grand Opera House and Hippodrome Cinema fame rang me up and asked if I'd heard of this thing called television. I said I had. Then he said I was now on his staff. He didn't ask me if I wanted that. George did not ask people. He simply told them what was to happen. George Lodge was with the Duke of Abercorn group and at the time was making a great error of judgement because he assumed that the television contract would really be awarded by the Stormont establishment. He said that they had Lord Wakehurst (the Governor of Northern Ireland) supporting them – as well as everybody who was anybody at that time.

And as it turned out, George Lodge was counting chickens ahead of time and his group lost. However, Gordon Duffield's interest in cinema made him an attractive proposition to any group trying to set up a television station. Cinema was looked upon as a first cousin to the emerging television. The *Kine Weekly*, originally named the *Kinematograph Weekly* when first published in 1889, was the prestigious journal of record for the cinema industry, and being its correspondent in Belfast accorded Gordon Duffield status in moving-picture circles and beyond. He also wrote on cinema topics for his own paper, the *Belfast Telegraph*. So perhaps he was not altogether surprised when the Ulster Television group contacted him in the person of Hubert 'Hibbie' Wilmot. 'Come and see Brum,' Hibbie said.

'Brum made an offer I could not refuse,' says Duffield. 'I was appointed to an ill-defined position which doubled my salary overnight from fifteen pounds a week to thirty pounds. I found myself with a very small group of people I already knew, among them Basil Lapworth, a former cinema manager appointed to look after advertising, and Hibbie in a shop front in Donegall Street with one telephone.' Brum described these temporary premises as small and rudimentary. His secretary indiscreetly went further to a *Daily Mail* journalist, describing her experience graphically as 'sitting in a garret with a drip on the end of my nose', a quote too delicious for the journalist to disregard. Brum recorded that when it appeared in print, Ivan Pollin, owner of the 'garret', was not impressed.

Finding a home for the station was the top priority. They knew that whatever they found, it would not be a television studio. The BBC owned the only television studio in Belfast, so an existing building would have to be adapted. In the months before the first transmission, no doubt Sydney Box continued advising his friend Bill MacQuitty to keep a tight rein on expenditure and to follow the Tyne Tees ITV example. The first ITV companies were having a financially difficult time. Tyne Tees, where Sydney was a director, went on air during the first month of Bill's contract as Ulster Television's managing director. It had bought a couple of furniture warehouses in Newcastle and converted them. They worked well and in fact the company remained in them until 2005.

Paddy Falloon, too, combed Belfast for suitable premises to convert. He found Havelock House, to the disappointment of Brum Henderson, who had been appointed Ulster Television's first general manager under Bill MacQuitty. Brum had favoured a site by the River Lagan opposite the Stranmillis teacher training college. However, the board ruled that out. There could be no question of building on a greenfield site for two good reasons. First, the shareholders did not have the money and secondly, they did not have the time to design, build and equip such a site before 31 October. The directors considered fifty-seven possibilities before settling on Havelock House, which was bought for £17,000. It was a derelict, late Victorian former hemstitching factory and warehouse on the Ormeau Road, a very solid building with iron pillars supporting spacious, adaptable areas. Havelock House was not in the city's business centre or modern leafy suburbs, but at the unfashionable end of the Ormeau Road, opposite the gasworks and next to terraced housing alongside a railway cutting. The board later promised to move to more salubrious custom-built premises along the Lagan, but that remained an aspiration. It nearly happened later, but in the end, UTV stayed where it was, expanding its footprint over the years.

MacQuitty had plenty of other considerations to keep him busy, not least talking and negotiating with electronics firms and managers about equipment and running requirements. The full weight of what lay before him was becoming apparent. 'I began to think I must have been mad ever to touch this venture,' he wrote afterwards. Eighty shareholders were putting up £100,000, with a call for twice that amount, and were becoming worried about the wisdom of their investment. Bill drew upon his film background. 'As with producing a film, the main task was to choose the best people. I settled on George Kelsey of Marconi for equipment; on Howard Steel of ABC to work with our architect, Brian Hewitt, to equip Havelock House. Gradually a magic forest of TV artefacts grew up through concealed floor ducts into an air-conditioned control room ingeniously fitted between the old building's iron-pillar supports. Two modest studios came into being, as did a small fixed-camera newsroom.'

UTV was not left entirely on its own during these trying initial months. The ITA worked on the 'buddy' system. They would ask an already established ITV company to chaperone and assist new companies to the point where they came on air, and thereby increase their chances of survival. The company helping UTV was ABC, full title Associated British Corporation (a name which was never used on air, just the initials). It had the franchise for the English midlands.

Havelock House in 1958, looking from what is now the UTV car park towards the Ormeau Road. You have to admire the foresight of the founders of UTV in buying this building in this condition and believing that it could be made into a television station in under a year.

Jokers in the fifties said ABC stood for All Bloody Commercials, so it was just the company to ask about setting up a London sales office. About three quarters of the revenue of UTV, perhaps more, was expected to come from advertisers who wanted a UK-wide exposure. These big advertisers would buy advertising on every company to achieve that. London offices were expensive and MacQuitty did not want to make the call for extra cash from already edgy shareholders. He talked the head of ABC, Howard Thomas, his chief mentor, into releasing his sales manager, Mike Hutcheson, for duty as head of UTV's London sales. In all, it was something of a raiding party on ABC. He also got from them Frank Brady as a chief engineer and SE Reynolds as a programme controller. Before joining ABC, Reynolds had worked at the BBC's Alexandra Palace, where British Television started. These were the key people MacQuitty needed. The rest, he decided, had to be recruited locally. This was not universally accepted by the rest of the board, particularly with regard to the crucial post of managing director. They felt that someone from England would be needed.

The Northern Ireland establishment of the time, well represented on the Ulster Television board, looked culturally, fraternally and (largely, though not exclusively) politically to England. Almost automatically the board members would consider that, in circumstances where all other qualities might be equal, the person from England would be better than the person from Northern Ireland. It is interesting to note that despite being the son of the managing director of the *Belfast Telegraph* and having been educated at Campbell College on the outskirts of Belfast, Bill MacQuitty was happy to

This was the author's first exposure on television, at the age of 17. He was taking part in a UTV schools quiz in 1960, in the school uniform of Portadown College. The team lost. The hair has not survived.

consider himself, and be regarded by others, as an Englishman, as evinced by his statement to putative board members when they were worried about the extent and weight of English shareholdings. MacQuitty told them he would be happy to restrict English participation to one quarter, within which he would number himself. Having made that point, with regard to the appointment of a managing director, it is also true that there would have been nobody at that time in Northern Ireland with any professional experience of running a commercial broadcasting organisation. Several likely candidates from across the water seemed interested, including Huw Weldon, who, according to Bill MacQuitty, had at that time an urge to leave the BBC and run his own show. Weldon was the editor of the very prestigious BBC arts television programme, 'Monitor'. He was also the programme's main interviewer and had a public profile. However, he was a BBC man through and through and had no commercial experience. Weldon, later Sir

A publicity shot of Adrienne McGuill at the time of UTV's launch.

Huw, hailed from north Wales and his only connection with Northern Ireland would have been a period of distinguished service with the Royal Ulster Rifles in World War II.

MacQuitty wrote of this time:

The more I thought about it, however, the more I was convinced that only an Ulsterman was going to be able to cope with Ulster politics. From that point of view, the choice narrowed down to Brum Henderson, MA of Trinity College, Dublin, who had worked on the *News Letter*, Ireland's oldest newspaper, and had a wide grasp of Ulster affairs. Against him was the fact that he was still only twenty-nine and had no previous experience of television, and that two of his family were already on the board. Moreover, he shared my instinctive reluctance to tie himself into an all-devouring and uncertain enterprise. In the end he accepted the situation, and his father, in a graceful gesture, resigned from the board in his favour.

So Brum Henderson, at the remarkably young age of 29, assumed the role of managing-director-in-waiting in May 1959, six months ahead of opening night. By this time, the reality of the financial situation was becoming more apparent to the board. Brum Henderson described what was happening inside the company:

It had been known from the outset that the company would have to pay an annual rental to the ITA of more than £100,000, a huge sum equivalent to half our total capitalisation. It had become clear also that our bid had seriously underestimated other costs, both in terms of capital spending in Belfast and of various services we would need to pay for when we were broadcasting. The prospect of profit appeared to be receding into a dim and uncertain future while the possibility of crippling losses seemed ever more real. In this climate, every penny spent on the embryonic station looked to many board members like money down the drain and the inevitable result was paralysis. We needed hard decisions.

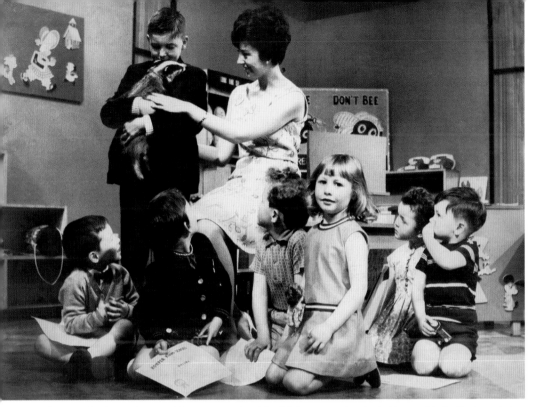

They say in the acting world, never work with children or animals. Adrienne McGuill at work in 'Romper Room' with both.

One of the ITV managing directors in England said to UTV that the way to make money in television was not to make programmes. This remains true today. Many of the plethora of digital stations presently broadcasting do not make or commission any programmes at all. They re-run programmes made by other stations in the past, sometimes the long-gone past, and can harvest an audience without owning any substantial studios. They have a small continuity sound studio, a bank of play-out machines and office space for their few sales, programme acquisition, finance and administration staff. Such TV stations, providing no live programming and no information, could be run from something the size of a mobile classroom and with very few people.

A similar path was not open to UTV or any ITV company. To win the contract, they had to show that they would provide a news service and public service programming. The aspirations in this regard of Ulster Television's contract application put together so enthusiastically in the Crawfordsburn Inn were proving to be financial millstones. The costings associated with programme targets had clearly been horribly over-optimistic. In the real world after the awarding of the contract, Ulster Television did not think it could not afford them. But cutting back was not easy.

It is evident that acrimonious discussions took place among board members and one casualty was 'Hibbie', or Hubert, Wilmot, the man who had phoned Gordon Duffield. Wilmot had been invited to join by Brum Henderson because of his theatre connections and was being spoken of at one time as the first programme controller. Hubert Wilmot and his wife, Dorothy, had gained a special affection among theatregoers in Belfast. The two of them started up a theatre club in 1944 and the enterprise grew to become the Belfast Arts Theatre, a purpose-built 450-seat theatre on Botanic Avenue, Belfast. But in 1959 Hubert Wilmot was watching the axe being taken to the programme strands in which he had a particular interest. He left, to return to his Arts Theatre. Meanwhile in Ulster Television, various weekly programme proposals were scrapped one after the other but the sums were still not coming out in the black. In the end the company decided that it could not even afford a news service. Programming was pulled back to an early-evening magazine programme, to be called 'Roundabout':

Brum put a brave face on it.

> Once the new plan was in place, however, a stark fact was evident: so much had been thrown out that apart from a few 'specials' sprinkled over the early months of broadcasting it looked as though local programmes would be limited to one single daily show. I put all our eggs in one basket and that basket was 'Roundabout'. This was a happy idea – good enough, we thought, to convince our viewers, our advertisers and our own staff (once we had one) that we really meant business. The origin of the show lay in the idea that even if we could not have news we could still make a contribution in current affairs. So we planned a programme which brought Ulster life in its many forms into our one small studio each night. The brief was wide, embracing the arts, business, agriculture, sport and matters of small-scale local interest as well as politics and general events, and the tone would be as relaxed and accessible as current television conventions allowed. Essentially a complement to the Belfast newspapers (which we shamelessly plundered for ideas), 'Roundabout' was to run for half an hour in a teatime slot every weekday.

■ Professor Jack Prichard (*right*) in the 'Midnight Oil' series, which was broadcast in July 1962. [Other man not known.] The programmes covered medicine, law, literature, music, physics, history and economics. The IBA was sufficiently impressed by them to contemplate seriously making Northern Ireland the area in which to experiment with an educational channel.

From 'Boatman Do Not Tarry', a play by John D. Stewart, in 1968. The actors are (l to r) Michael Duffy, Paddy McIlhenny, Louis Rolston, Jimmy Devlin (in car) and Sean Reid. Jimmy Devlin could not drive, so for certain shots the car was pulled by an unseen tow rope!

Brum Henderson wrote that he believed this single offering, 'Roundabout', would be good enough to convince viewers and advertisers and his own staff. This was classic 'Brum-speak'. The staff consent would be easy. The company had no staff, or very few. Nor were there any viewers as yet. Prospective viewers' expectations with respect to local programming would have been low. Their yardstick would have been television from BBC Northern Ireland, which was providing a modest 5 minutes a weekday at 6.10 p.m. each evening. Prospective advertisers would not worry for two reasons. The great majority of programming on Ulster Television was to be network and therefore the majority of advertising space would be within networked programmes, not local. Furthermore, the majority of advertisers would be from outside the province and they would not care very much about local programmes.

Conspicuously absent from Brum's list of those to be convinced were the people in the ITA who had awarded his company the contract. Having once worked for one of the ITA's successor bodies, I can imagine how badly this development would have gone down with the regulator. The Northern Ireland programme contract had been won competitively on the basis of a series of programme promises to the ITA. Once approved by the ITA, part of their brief was to fulfil the regulator's requirement for public service elements in the programme schedule, as required by the 1954 Television Act. Remember, the proposals by the Cunninghams and the Duke of Abercorn had been rejected in favour of those of Ulster Television – who were now effectively tearing them up. If pushed, the ITA could have declared Ulster in default of its promises and awarded the contract to the Cunninghams, or re-advertised it.

Lord Antrim, as chairman, wrote to the ITA to tell it what was happening. When he read the letter, the Director General of the ITA, Sir Robert Frazer, ordered Bill MacQuitty over to London to explain. Brum Henderson went with him. Frazer was a forceful Australian and a plain speaker. Brum referred to the meeting as a 'grilling'. Lord Antrim's letter had complained about the £100,000 annual payment to the ITA, saying that it was too high. He had argued that it had been calculated on the population formula adopted elsewhere in the system, but that it was unfair to apply it to Northern Ireland. While Northern Ireland had a population of about one and a half million, the proportion owning television sets

Helen Madden, the second presenter of 'Romper Room', is pictured here with the magic mirror through which she brought her young audience into a make-believe world.

was far lower than, for example, the proportion in the south of England. It was thought that there were about 80,000 television sets in Northern Ireland around 1958. The number of sets was the important figure, argued Antrim, because the company's revenue projections had to be based on the potential reach of the programmes.

Sir Robert threw that argument out. He said that the number of television sets in Northern Ireland was either the same as or slightly higher than when they had submitted their application and their programme proposals. He was particularly angry about losing local news and told Brum Henderson that he was disappointed to hear such a proposal from someone with a newspaper background. MacQuitty and Henderson pleaded and argued that the company might well go under if the

ITA stuck to its position. But the loss of local news would lay the ITA open to the accusation that it was soft on the public service requirements of the licence contract. The provision of a local news service as a counterbalance to the BBC news service had been a main public service requirement in setting up independent television.

Oddly, a BBC television programme came to the aid of the hapless pair that day. The Ulster Television men talked up the 'Roundabout' proposal, saying that it was to be a local version of the BBC's 'Tonight' programme. It was a good move, perhaps the one that tipped the balance. 'Tonight' was a new-style magazine programme, informally presented by Cliff Mitchelmore, on which some impressive reporting talent was cutting its teeth. One such reporter was Alan Whicker, later a founder shareholder of Yorkshire Television, and presenter of the fabled 'Whicker's World' TV programmes. Unusually for the BBC, 'Tonight' was irreverent and piecemeal, mixing light and heavy, which suited the audience available between 6.00 p.m. and 7.00 p.m. Furthermore, the programme was seen as a successful riposte by the BBC against the incursions of the new ITV, which had succeeded in grabbing almost three quarters of the audience. At its peak, 'Tonight' achieved an audience of seven million viewers.

A 'Romper Room' give-away mug extolling the virtues of drinking milk. Milk was given free to schoolchildren in the UK in the sixties and perhaps because of this many children did not value it sufficiently.

Sir Robert would have been aware of the success of the 'Tonight' format and nobody else in the ITV system had as yet proposed doing something similar. Sensing that they were making headway, the UTV men said 'Roundabout' would contain serious material as well as lighter, and it would help stamp a local identity on the station. Sir Robert relented, as Brum Henderson relates: 'A little grudgingly, he gave it his blessing on the condition that we undertook to handle real, hard news in 'Roundabout' if big stories broke. He emphasized that this dispensation was temporary and that he expected a gradual increase in our output and, in particular, the introduction of a news service as soon as income permitted. Naturally we agreed.'

One other factor played into their hands. Ulster was the smallest station the ITA had decided to proceed with. If it had foreclosed on Ulster Television because of its retreat on the public service requirements, it was by no means certain that a new application with similar aspirations would emerge as a replacement. In fact, it might take some time before another application appeared. Perhaps there would be none. The ITA also had a duty to get ITV started and, having done so, to ensure the stability of the system. Knowing something of the regulatory system from within, I would guess that Sir Robert and his colleagues at the ITA had decided that if UTV were just postponing their proposals until the financial climate brightened, they could live with that. Bill MacQuitty and Brum Henderson got what they needed, but they were left in no doubt that if the scaling down of local programmes proved to be a device for increasing profits, the ITA would act against them severely.

In today's world, where the successor regulator of ITV is reducing public service requirements from companies, the importance of imposing them during these formative years of ITV might not be fully appreciated. The context of broadcasting in the fifties was very different. Politicians worried about broadcasting and meddled, precisely because it intruded into the home. Public service broadcasting was represented as an essential ingredient in the British way of life. It made British broadcasting different. It was well regarded in many parts of the world, which is why Britain was being very careful not to create a broadcasting structure which would undermine that achievement.

The BBC 'Tonight' programme itself illustrates this thinking. It is scarcely believable today that television in the late forties and for most of the fifties shut down between six and seven every evening except on Sundays, so that small children throughout the land could be put to bed – perhaps the most explicit manifestation ever of the nanny state. The BBC introduced this hour of blank screens when television opened up again after World War II. It went unremarked until ITV began in 1955 and found the money was not coming in as fast as envisaged. When the BBC was not broadcasting, it was saving money; when an independent company was not broadcasting, it could be losing money. No advertisements, no revenue. So the ITA joined cause with the TV companies in working towards an end to the 'Toddlers' Truce', as it was called. Nothing happened about it until Charles Hill became Postmaster General, the minister in charge of broadcasting, and who in later years was to be appointed chairman of the ITA. Hill was no friend of the BBC and thought the Toddlers' Truce was nonsense and a piece of BBC paternalism. He later said, 'This restriction seemed to me absurd and I said so. It was the responsibility of parents, not the state, to put their children to bed at the right time . . . I invited the BBC and the ITA to agree to its abolition.' The BBC was reluctant but Hill got it abolished in February 1957. The BBC first put a pop programme, 'Six Five Special', into the slot, then, soon after, the 'Tonight' programme. The abolition of the Toddler's Truce was not an end to restriction on the number of hours television could broadcast. That freedom had to wait until 1972.

So the 'Tonight' programme helped spawn 'Roundabout', which was to be the first nightly magazine programme on British regional television, whether BBC or ITV. And in Sir Robert Frazer's office that day in 1959, 'Roundabout' gave Ulster Television the breathing space it desperately needed.

Chapter 3

The original master control in the early sixties at Havelock House. A young Eric Caves (*left*) is pictured with Frank Holmes, technical supervisor. Eric would be conducting sound control and engineering checks and Frank was the vision switcher. In the small continuity studio is Adrienne McGuill.

The place UTV was born into

In the fifties BBC NI news was fighting to achieve acknowledged independence from government and from the Stormont government in particular. In the mid-fifties, the BBC recruited its first television journalist, a man from Larne called Cecil Taylor, who had experience of reporting for the *News Letter* and *The Irish Times*. Note that the BBC interviewing panel which recruited him included the Northern Ireland Civil Service Commissioner. As BBC historian Jonathan Bardon records, when Taylor was asked his opinion of the BBC news bulletins, he replied that they sounded 'as if they were written by night at the Northern Ireland Press Office in Stormont and that they were being broadcast by the BBC for the benefit of the Protestant and Unionist population, ignoring the minority'. Taylor got the job and rose to the highest levels of the BBC in Northern Ireland. I worked under him and can testify that he strove to maintain a non-partisan ethic in broadcasting, sometimes to his own considerable personal cost.

This kind of integrity was desperately needed by the end of the fifties in all broadcasting, which was an additional reason why the ITA received the news of Ulster Television's withdrawal of a news service so badly. Ulster Television's bulletins were to provide a much-needed new editorial standpoint. At the time there were four daily newspapers circulating, the *Belfast Telegraph*, the *News Letter* and the *Northern Whig* – all Unionist in various shades – and the *Irish News*, which was the single daily nationalist paper. I suspect that Cecil Taylor wanted broadcast news competition from Ulster Television as soon as possible for the good of the BBC and his own peace of mind.

Another often forgotten context to the beginning of Ulster Television was the campaign of violence by the IRA and allied organisations between 1956 and 1962. It was a desultory effort which concentrated on the border customs posts. These posts were a feature on the approved roads across the border, the most noted being at Killeen on the main road between Belfast and Dublin. It was bombed on a number of occasions at night, when it was unoccupied, and often at weekends. When the *News Letter* was still a broadsheet, one wit in the sub-editors' room discovered he could fit a double headline across the front page in a 36-point Century Bold typeface which read, 'Friday Night is Gelignite'.

It was not submitted to the editor for consideration. The campaign of violence petered out in early 1963, but not before the BBC transmitter above Londonderry had been bombed. The directors of Ulster Television would have known that setting up a commercial television station was not like setting up any other type of business. Television was special and it could have enemies as well as friends. Brum Henderson revealed how sensitive certain issues were politically. Frank Brady had been recruited as chief engineer by Ulster Television from the staff of ABC, one of quite a number taken from that company because their television expertise was badly needed. Frank was a Catholic from Navan in the Irish Republic and, in accordance with the law of the time, he needed a work permit. This was before the free movement of labour enjoyed under the European Union. Work permits in Northern Ireland were only given by the government at Stormont, which was Unionist-dominated, if a local person with the required skills was not available. There was a delay with the issuing of Frank's permit and eventually Brum was sent for personally by the Minister for Development at Stormont, Major

Spot Advertisement Rates

Effective from Monday, 21st September, 1964

Weekdays		Before 5.30 G	5.30–6.00 E	6.00–7.00 B	7.00–10.25 A	10.25–11.05 D	11.05–Close F
	60 seconds	£20	£70	£120	£160	£100	£50
	45 seconds	£15	£53	£90	£120	£75	£38
	30 seconds	£10	£35	£60	£80	£50	£25
	15 seconds	£7	£23	£40	£53	£33	£17

Saturday		Before 4.00 G	4.00–6.00 F	6.00–11.00 C	11.00–11.30 E	11.30–Close G
	60 seconds	£20	£50	£110	£70	£20
	45 seconds	£15	£38	£83	£53	£15
	30 seconds	£10	£25	£55	£35	£10
	15 seconds	£7	£17	£37	£23	£7

Sunday		Before 3.00 G	3.00–4.30 F	4.30–7.25 E	7.25–8.15 C	8.15–10.40 AA	10.40–11.15 C	11.15–Close G
	60 seconds	£20	£50	£70	£110	£180	£110	£20
	45 seconds	£15	£38	£53	£83	£135	£83	£15
	30 seconds	£10	£25	£35	£55	£90	£55	£10
	15 seconds	£7	£17	£23	£37	£60	£37	£7

An advertising rate card from 1964. For comparison, prices 45 years on are: £2,200 for 60 seconds, and £1,100 for 30 seconds.

Ivan Neill, to account for the choice. Brum believed that a member of the UTV board had alerted Stormont to the fact that Frank Brady was a Catholic from south of the border. In Brum's words, the episode ended thus: 'Neill, to his credit, was clearly embarrassed and unhesitatingly accepted my assurance that people with experience in television engineering were in such short supply that local preference was simply not possible. The permit was duly issued.'

Both the bids for the independent television licence could be viewed as one of the last genuflections in the direction of an age of deference and social stratification that was fading. Both the applications were headed by aristocracy, the unsuccessful one by the Duke of Abercorn and the winner by the Earl of Antrim. It was obviously felt by the commercial interests in the two groupings that having them headed by titled people and 'old money' added to the lustre of the undertakings. One day, around the time of the applications, some Ulster Television directors were in the Pig 'n Chicken restaurant, then owned by Cyril Lord, a carpet tycoon. One of them suggested that Cyril Lord be asked to join the board. According to Brum Henderson, Ivan Pollin retorted: 'No way, we are over-lorded already.' By now they had on board Lord Antrim and Lord O'Neil and had also approached Lord Dunleath, who eventually declined. Contrast this with the bids to the regulator for commercial radio in the seventies and later. There were no lords in these delegations. Half a century later, there are no lords, ladies, dukes or earls on the Ulster Television board of directors.

In 1959, Northern Ireland, Britain and western Europe were on the verge of the Swinging Sixties, which finally demolished the long age of reverence. During Ulster Television's first decade, pop culture and the space age would emerge. Three weeks before the station launched, the robotic Soviet probe Luna-3 returned by means of a television signal the first images of the dark side of the moon. The approaching decades would reveal, also largely by television, the dark side of Northern Ireland in the form of the Troubles, which would be the backdrop to much of UTV's first half-century.

There are fewer and fewer people around who remember society before television and experienced what it was like as this new medium spread rapidly into homes across Northern Ireland. One of the most knowledgable of those who do is Derek Martin, who, now retired, lives in Newtownabbey outside Belfast. Some might remember him as DV Martin, retailer of television sets in Monkstown and Whiteabbey, near Belfast. He was President of the Radio and Television Retailers' Association in 1980, when that organisation held Northern Ireland's last radio and television show in the King's Hall. The event was sponsored by Ulster Television, which broadcast live from the venue. It is a sign of what has happened with television that nobody would think today of staging such a show.

The early part of Derek Martin's life is a snapshot of when Northern Ireland was moving into the television age. The advent of television and Ulster Television was a shared experience for everybody in Northern Ireland, whether or not they were able to own a set.

Waiting in the wings for the moment was a small band of enthusiasts, and one of them was Derek. Northern Ireland used to be a powerhouse in linen manufacture but by the 1950s, those old industries were in decline. The Dublin Road in Belfast still housed linen concerns, such as the damask design building of John Shaw Brown & Sons, now the site of a multiscreen cinema. This is where Derek worked, a skilful artist designing damask. As a basis for a career in electronics, this was out of the ordinary, even by the standards of the day.

■ The 'Sportsbeat' team in the late eighties: Jackie Fullerton, Jacqui Berkley and Adrian Logan.

But there was a link between electronics and Derek's early days. His father had settled in Jordanstown, where he built the bungalow in which Derek was born. This was a time when electricity was not in every home and Derek's father charged accumulators as a sideline. A word of explanation for those born after the middle of the last century. Accumulators were a type of lead-acid battery often used to power radios in homes without electricity, and there were plenty of those in the thirties. At that time, town gas from coal and electricity were battling it out as energy sources. You could have a gas-powered radio, believe it or not. The Milnes Company in Yorkshire invented a thermo-generator for powering radio receivers. It generated electricity from gas by heating thermocouples, albeit inefficiently, and this was marketed as an alternative to accumulators. (There is a thermo-generator on display in the Flame Gasworks Museum of Ireland in Carrickfergus, Co. Antrim, the only such museum in Ireland.)

The Martin bungalow had electricity, and in the garage Mr Martin Senior installed what was known as a Davenset board: an accumulator charging set, which used mains electricity to charge banks of accumulators. Derek recalls its operation: 'People usually had two accumulators, which were glass receptacles with terminals. While one was charging, you used the other. Even today people say to me that they remember their fathers coming to mine to get their batteries charged, some walking from Greenisland. On the Davenset board there was a big rheostat so that you could keep the charging current adjusted to a certain level, no matter how many batteries were charging at the time.' Derek himself learnt to do this as a boy, and from that a fascination with electrical gadgets grew. However, there was no clear career path in that direction, and Derek's father helped get him a job in linen in the design department, a well regarded post in its day: 'When I started working I got only four pounds a week and I had to hand that to my mother. She handed me back a shilling – that's five pence in today's currency – a day for my lunch. Rather than buy a lunch, some days I would buy a component from a small wholesalers near the Technical College called Electrical Agencies. I was fascinated by all these condensers and such like. Electronics must have been in my blood. The linen industry was not.'

One day Derek read a newspaper article about a man named Hull who had a television set in the days before television in any form had reached Northern

Ireland. Derek headed off unannounced to see this man at his home at the top of the Springfield Road in Belfast, which is well up the side of Black Mountain, overlooking the city. 'The house could be identified by the big aerial on the roof. Mr Hull received me kindly and brought me to this tiny television set. The picture was snowy, but good enough to see that it was a courtroom drama featuring actors in legal wigs,' says Derek. This wonder of the modern age was possible because of the position of Mr Hull's home. From his high position, he was able to receive television from the Holme Moss transmitter to the east of Manchester in the Pennines. That transmitter was 170 miles from Belfast in a straight line, and Mr Hull had done well to receive the signal, given that the normal range of these transmitters was 30 to 40 miles. The mast at Holme Moss had been built in 1951 to transmit BBC television on VHF on 405 lines, black and white.

Derek Martin still vividly remembers seeing that first television picture in the early fifties, and recalls the impact it made upon him: 'I had well and truly caught the bug but there was no way I could have afforded a TV set. Televisions cost about fifty or sixty pounds and my weekly wage had only risen to seven or eight pounds at the time. So I decided to build one.'

To do that, there were two prerequisites for Derek: the detailed knowledge and the parts. The knowledge came from a magazine produced by an extraordinary character called FJ Camm, brother of Sydney Camm, who designed the Hurricane fighter plane. FJ Camm was also an engineer and an inveterate hobbyist and journalist. He was editor of *Practical Wireless* magazine, from which Derek learnt about building a television set.

This was where World War II came in handy, since in the fifties there was still plenty of World War II detritus on the market. During the war, IFF was developed – Identification Friend or Foe. It was a system that enabled an aircraft to identify itself as a friend in response to a coded signal. Derek used an IFF set as a main component of his homemade set – and it worked.

In the fifties, retailers sold radios and then television sets as an adjunct to other businesses. Shops survived by selling radios in the winter and bicycles in the summer. It was to one of these hybrid retailers that Derek first went, a garage owner who was selling television sets in a small shop as a sideline. But within the year, Derek had moved to the Belfast firm of Len Ferris at the corner of My Lady's

Road and Ravenhill Road and remained there for five years: 'I was thrown into the deep end, not only selling televisions, but installing them, servicing them and repairing them. With those early sets I was receiving up to a dozen service calls about faulty sets. Brum Henderson had at that time a holiday home at Brown's Bay, Islandmagee. The coastline of the bay is on the Antrim coast which is backed by high land, so he was unable to receive television signals from Northern Ireland. Therefore he had an aerial installed to receive signals from Scotland – an installation by Derek Martin.'

Derek worked in conditions that would appal present health and safety officials: 'I would be sent alone up the Springfield Road on a winter night in the snow to put up an aerial on a three-storey building. Tuning in the aerials was critical. I was frightened of slipping over the edge while on the roof. I had to make the adjustments to the aerial, unable to shout down to anyone watching a picture to see if it needed more adjustment. Eventually I developed my own little device with earphones for picking up the signal to adjust rooftop aerials.'

In modern electronics, repairs are often effected by simply removing a circuit board and replacing it. But half a century ago, you fixed it. One of the frequent faults in television sets was the dry solder joint. Solder was used to connect components as both a mechanical joint and, most importantly, an electrical joint. If the joint was disturbed while the solder was solidifying, the joint might either not conduct at all, or conduct very badly. It might also be sensitive to vibration or movement. When this happened, it was called a dry joint – and finding these joints was a problem. They were usually not detectable to the eye.

The method of locating these joints was literally hair-raising. It was done by hand with the electricity flowing. 'I had the reputation of being very good at finding dry joints,' says Derek, 'and I received many electrical shocks working on radios. We would find where the voltage stopped by touching the wires with the wet fingers. I learnt to work with one hand, so that if I did touch a live component, the shock did not go through my body.'

Today we simply turn on a television set and, other than changing channels on the remote, there is nothing else to do. This was not the case with early sets. There was no remote, of course, although a wired remote control called, appropriately enough, 'Lazy Bones' had been developed. But numeric pad infra-red remote controls as we know them did not appear until the eighties. The first cathode ray tube sets, as well as tuning, had a multitude of controls – horizontal hold, vertical hold, contrast, brightness. They might have all needed tweaking on a daily basis. Derek can recall the coronation of Queen Elizabeth being televised on 2 June 1953. The pictures came from a temporary BBC transmitter in the Glencairn area of Belfast. One of those manning that transmitter was a young engineer called Eric Caves, destined to become the chief engineer of Ulster Television. Neighbours and relatives headed for the homes of those with sets to watch television for the first time. 'On that day of the Coronation, people were in their houses in darkened rooms with the blinds down and all their friends sitting on the floor,' Derek remembers. 'Some of them were always going up to the television to adjust the contrast or brightness. Then others would crawl over and poke at the controls, saying, "I think that's a wee bit better now." And everybody else would be bawling, "Leave it alone, it's alright now."'

Eventually Derek set up in business himself in Monkstown. As his shop was being built, he remembers with pride the notice on the site: 'New premises for DV Martin', and when it came to an opening ceremony, he secured the services of TV presenter Sally Ogle, one of Northern Ireland's first television celebrities, who eventually left to set up home with her husband in California. When Ulster Television started, DV Martin sold a lot more television sets. He was appointed the UTV monitor for the Carnmoney Hill transmitter, which could not be received at Havelock House. If a viewer reported a failure of the television signal in the Monkstown area, which once happened more frequently than now, UTV would phone Derek to see if the transmitter was working or not, because many viewers assumed that if their picture disappeared, it could not possibly be their own TV set at fault.

Today, as you might expect, Derek has a large, state-of-the-art widescreen flat panel television set, which he sometimes views using a wireless stereophonic headset. He remains an ardent television and electronics enthusiast and a link to days gone forever.

Chapter 4

First night at the Fun Factory

In 1959 the European Broadcasting Union was only nine years old and the ITA, among others, mounted a conference to impress this new organisation with the achievements of independent broadcasting in the UK. Every ITV company was expected to come up with programme material to impress the Europeans. Ulster Television could well have done without this in the run-up to its launch and said so, but the ITA was insistent. The other companies were rolling out worthy productions of Shakespeare, ballet, orchestral performances, operas. UTV had nothing to show.

Bill MacQuitty tells of coming up with a simple device for the conference. He decided to talk about the station in front of a map, because in those days nobody knew where Ulster was. In his talk, MacQuitty referred to the lack of television sets in Northern Ireland, which by then was not strictly true, but it made for a good story. He said that one day he saw a television aerial on the roof of a thatched cottage in the Mountains of Mourne. He was invited inside, as he recounts:

'Do you like it?' I asked the owner.

'Man,' he said, 'if ye shut yer eyes it's every bit as good as the wireless.'

I asked the wife what she thought. 'Ah,' she said, 'it's well enough, it keeps the ould fella quiet, but it's a terrible bad light for reading by.'

The Europeans seemed to love this stage-Irish folksy contribution more than the more sophisticated offerings, reinforcing as it undoubtedly did their stereotypical image of the place.

The next hurdle for the Ulster Television team would be the launch and attendant festivities, some of which would have continued to reinforce an Irish stereotype. The day before the big day, the members of the ITA, led by chairman Sir Ivone Kirkpatrick, along with various London-based members of the Ulster Television board, shared a plane over to Nutts Corner, which was then the main airport in Northern Ireland. Things unravelled somewhat. It began when board member and actress, Bea Lillie, arrived late and somewhat drunk with her companion, John Huck. She always introduced him with: 'That's Huck with an H.' During the flight, Bea tottered up and down the aisle, singing 'Does Your Mother Come from Ireland?' to Sir Ivone and the other ITA members. Some were embarrassed.

When the plane landed, there was a power cut and in the murk, Bea Lillie missed her footing on the aircraft steps and fell into the arms of Brum Henderson, who was waiting at the bottom. In those less security-conscious days, you could meet people at the aircraft if you had enough clout. Also on the aircraft was Sir Laurence Olivier, who was a UTV director and special guest. He watched a string of Rolls-Royce limos approach the aircraft to take the ITA chairman and members to Hillsborough Castle, or 'Government House', as it was then known, where they were to stay with the Northern Ireland Governor, Lord Wakehurst. As Olivier waited ever longer, he became tetchy. MacQuitty had told Brum to have Rolls-Royces for the company VIPs, but by the time he had got round to it, the

Governor's staff had hired all that were available. In the words of MacQuitty, the best Brum could come up with for Sir Laurence and other board members were 'ancient Pontiacs stained with years of marriages and funerals, and smelling of drink and vomit'. When Sir Laurence emerged from his sub-prime limo and entered the Grand Central Hotel in Belfast's Royal Avenue, the receptionist asked him who he was. It was explained to her that this was the famous Sir Laurence who had arrived to open the new television station, whereupon the girl told him he looked nothing like his picture. Brum, in his memoirs, refers to the whole sequence of events as 'bizarre'.

The next day, Hallowe'en, proceedings began with a celebratory lunch hosted by Sir Ivone and the ITA at the Grand Central. In his speech, the Northern Ireland Prime Minister welcomed the advent of UTV as 'a vote of confidence in the stability of the Northern Ireland government'. It was no such vote, but Sir Ivone would not have chosen that moment to contradict him.

After lunch, the ITA and others headed for Havelock House. Adrienne McGuill travelled from her home in Belfast to Havelock House that afternoon on a bus. In a bag she carried the dress she would change into before she started work, bought specially and expensively for £20. Adrienne was on her way to being the first announcer on Ulster Television screens. When she entered the building she could hardly believe it was the same Havelock House she had been in the day before, when the place had seemed to be a shambles – builders, painters, ladders and debris everywhere. It was evident to her that even though the workmen had been toiling all night, they had not yet finished and the station was about to go on air. As she approached the door, paving stones were still being laid. But all of this was to be off-camera. The studios were ready, the gallery behind the glass for the television production staff was ready and the technical areas were ready. And she was ready. This was the biggest night of her young life, for she would be performing in front of her biggest audience.

But not her first audience. Adrienne McGuill was an actress. Before she left school, she had appeared on radio for BBC Belfast. 'Children's Hour', a late-afternoon radio programme, had a healthy audience among the young. That was before television demolished practically all children's programming on radio. Cicely Mathews, who holds a revered status among theatrical people and older broadcasters, was the presenter and organiser of the programme in Belfast and is credited with beginning the careers of many noted actors and broadcasters through her feature, 'I Want To Be an Actor'. Adrienne appeared on several occasions, reinforcing her determination to go into the theatre.

After leaving school, she went to the Guildhall School of Music and Drama in London and her future seemed mapped out for at least a few years. But not so. Adrienne had been forceful enough to manage to get to drama school, but there were family strains because of it. She was an only child and her mother was never happy about her going to London. Furthermore, it was costing her parents a fortune to foster her ambitions. There was no grant for drama school and London is an expensive city. She came back for the summer break after a successful first year and took a job in Hibbie Wilmot's Arts Theatre in Belfast. She remembers Hibbie as being a forthright, forceful person, probably a necessary prerequisite for survival in professional theatre in Belfast.

He was certainly forthright to Adrienne. He told her that there was not much point in giving her a job if she was going to disappear back to London after a couple of months. She didn't promise anything, but it might have crossed her mind that Hibbie's script that day could have been written by her mother. Hibbie gave her a stage-managing job at £3 15s a week (out of which she gave her mother £1). What remained in her pocket did not go too far, but the job was wonderful experience. Hibbie was gambling that once this young woman had breathed the air of real theatre, there was a chance she would stay. He was right. 'I initially thought it was a holiday job and thought I could simply go back to London if I wanted to,' Adrienne told me. 'But after a couple of months at the theatre, I found I was loving it all – the stage-managing, making the tea, prompting, scripting, everything. Eventually I began getting small parts in plays, usually a maid or something like that. It began to dawn on me that after I had qualified from drama school, this would be just the kind of job I wanted – so why go back to London?'

With commitment came bigger parts, including the lead in *Bus Stop*, a play by the American playwright William Inge, set in small-town mid-western America. A film based on the play of the same name was released in 1956 with Marilyn Monroe in the lead part. This coloured audience expectations of how the leading lady should look and to resemble Marilyn, Adrienne was required to dye her dark hair blonde. Her father was not pleased.

■ Adrienne McGuill, the original producer and presenter of the pre-school programme 'Romper Room' in the sixties.

Not long after, she saw the newspaper advertisement which changed the direction of her life. It was for on-screen posts in UTV and Adrienne decided to apply. 'I already knew a lot of Ulster Television people because they were theatregoers,' she says. 'I had done radio plays with Ronnie Mason, the BBC drama producer in Belfast, had been to drama school and worked in theatre, so I believed I had as good a CV as anybody could have.' But true to form, she was leaving as little as possible to chance and strengthened her credentials by travelling to Manchester and Granada Television to see what a continuity studio looked like. At Granada she was shown the ropes by no less than Noele Gordon, who was then a continuity announcer, but went on to become nationally famous in the mid-sixties playing the central character, Meg Richardson, in the soap, 'Crossroads'. Many will remember 'Crossroads' as a popular early-evening programme centred on a motel. It was mocked by critics for having a set with wobbly walls and lots of silent extras

as motel guests. Notwithstanding its popularity, in 1967 the ITA intervened to require it to go down from five nights a week to four in the hope that by relieving pressure on both production staff and cast, the quality of 'Crossroads' would improve. In those far-off days, regulators could bare their teeth at ITV programme companies to demand quality.

Adrienne was called for interview and now her problem was her Marilyn Monroe look. She concluded, and her father must have agreed, that UTV might be wanting a girl-next-door look and that the blonde-bombshell image had to go. So it was back to the hair dye again, this time a sober black. Havelock House was in the midst of a major interior rebuild when Adrienne presented herself for the first interview. Entrance was by the fire escape and through the typing pool. On the other side of the table were SE Reynolds, the programme controller, Colin Lecky Thompson, producer, Gordon Duffield, publicity manager and Brum Henderson, general manager. They liked what they saw and called her back for a screen test in a tiny studio, not much bigger than a couple of telephone boxes. The test script included the name of Reginald Bosanquet, the ITN reporter and later newsreader, and she stumbled over it. Reginald would surely have approved. He stumbled over many a word himself live on air. He was a much loved character reputed to have been asked once by a colleague where he was going, while leaving the green room in ITN with a glass of wine. He replied that he was off to read the news. Adrienne's interviewing panel disregarded the falter and she was appointed to one of the announcer jobs. Jimmy Greene and Brian Durkin got the others. There were two other appointments made at roughly the same time. Ivor Mills and Anne Gregg became the presenters of the new 'Roundabout' programme. As the sports presenter on 'Roundabout', they chose Ernie Strathdee, a former rugby star who played for the great Irish Triple Crown side of 1948.

Those appointed could justifiably pat themselves on the back. They interviewed 800 people for jobs in all parts of the company and of those, about eighty had had potential as presenters.

Meanwhile, behind the scenes, other parts of the jigsaw were falling into place. At the BBC the young engineer Eric Caves, destined to become UTV's chief engineer and who had been manning the transmitter which brought the first television pictures to Northern Ireland, had heard an unwelcome whisper that he

Robert Lamrock of UTV holds in his right hand the enormous tape cassette of the original video recorders at Havelock House. The small tape in his other hand is the equivalent of half a century later. The technology now is moving towards recording on a solid electronic chip.

might be transferred by the BBC to Wick in the far north of Scotland, on the North Sea coast – about 300 miles northwards in a straight line. He did not want to go, so when he saw engineering jobs for Ulster Television advertised, he shot in an application and was appointed as an assistant engineer. This was in September 1959, only six weeks before the start-up date of 31 October.

Eric was not a studio engineer. He was a transmitter engineer and had never seen a studio. 'To myself, who had spent five years with BBC transmitters, to come down into a studio environment was completely strange,' he says. 'Ten of us started on the twelfth of September. Havelock House was all bricks and mortar and cement, with a lot of building work going on. We were stepping over planks and there was dust everywhere. Ulster Television had brought over three senior engineers from ABC Manchester and they trained us over those six weeks, because we had little idea of the workings of sixteen millimetre or thirty-five millimetre projectors.' These were the machines through which all the film shot for the programmes would begin a first journey into people's homes.

The training was hectic because time was so short. At times it was very robust. Eric remembered the technique of one of the trainers, Frank Holmes. While they were training on the 16 mm projector, Frank would nip behind and stop it working, sometimes by breaking the film while it was running. He then stood back to see how the trainee engineers coped.

By the standards of today, the equipment was crude. A good example was how pictures on film were transformed into electronic pictures. It was done in the simplest possible way. In a device called a telecine, the film was projected straight into an electronic camera tube. However, these cameras were big and expensive and UTV could not afford to have one dedicated to a 35 mm slide projector, another to a 16 mm movie projector and yet another to a 35 mm movie projector. So the engineers used a mirror. They had a single electronic camera and the three projectors placed at various angles in front of it. A mirror, which could be directed easily into one of three preset positions, diverted the pictures from the desired projector into the TV tube. Simple, effective and cheap.

An even cheaper technique was used to solve another problem. There was no way of recording electronic pictures when Ulster Television started. That advance came in the early sixties, so film was of paramount importance. Film from different sources, especially speedily shot news film, varied in exposure and therefore density, so when its output from the mirror machine was running through the mixing desk, the engineers monitored it and had two controls to keep the pictures looking as they should. One knob controlled black level and the other was for contrast. However, some film was negative stock, so everything was the other way round. When negative film was running, therefore, the engineers crossed over their hands on the knobs and operated them that way.

But there was one technical problem that there was no easy and cheap way round. Havelock House is just opposite the Belfast Gasworks. Today the gasworks site is a 12-hectare home to a diverse range of organisations and modern businesses. With its access to the Lagan towpath for walkers and cyclists, it is an attractive and evocative place, particularly because it retains some of the original gasworks buildings, including the clock tower and the Klondike venue. The area is a monument to modernity, as it was in 1823, when the works opened to produce coal gas for Belfast. For the next 150 years, the gasworks provided light, heat and energy for industry, commerce and homes, and coal gas was therefore a factor in the great advances made by the city during the Industrial Revolution. At its zenith, the gasworks provided up to 2,000 people with an income and was generally regarded as one of the better employers. That is not to underplay some of the place's less attractive features. Producing gas was a 24-hour process and the gasworks was a never-endingly hot, noisy and filthy place of work. Among other components, coal gas contains carbon monoxide, sulphur, ammonia and tar, rendering it a poisonous concoction with the odour of rotten eggs. Despite this, mothers used to bring babies with whooping cough to the gasworks in the belief that allowing the infants to breathe the fumes would help. By the way, it was not the gas itself that was being inhaled, but the fumes emanating from the coal being consumed in gas retorts.

The fumes did the babies no favours and the same was true for some of the mechanisms inside Havelock House. The rotten-egg smell came from hydrogen sulphide, which causes corrosion within electronics even at low levels. Eric Caves explained what was happening:

> The technical equipment used valves and relays as well as transistors. The main master desk had lots and lots of relays. But being across the road from the gasworks, the vapours affected the contacts in the relays and eventually

stopped them working. We tried to close off the racks to keep the fumes out but we could not seal them. The valves and equipment inevitably created heat, which had to be dissipated. That meant we still had to have open vents to allow in cooling air but that also admitted the gasworks fumes. Nobody thought about that when they chose Havelock House. The gasworks closed in 1968 and that finally solved the problem.

Until then, the engineers kept a handy supply of spare relays to hand, ready for a quick substitution when the fumes did their work. Meanwhile, they rehearsed and rehearsed the technical arrangements until they felt confident that, short of a catastrophic component failure, it would be all right on the night.

The front-of-camera people had been doing much the same. For weeks on end, Adrienne McGuill turned up at Havelock House for rehearsal in the small continuity studio. To simulate programming, they had a war film which was cut up to allow advertising breaks. 'We had to read commercials over slides, do weather forecasts and talk about a mythical programme from our own scripts,' Adrienne recalls. 'I was always jealous of Anne Gregg and Ivor Mills because SE Reynolds would take them to his office after the rehearsed programme and debrief them. But nobody talked to us. Those two were doing programmes and therefore were more highly regarded.'

Announcing might look easy but it is a specific skill and very few television stations now feature in-vision announcing. UTV is possibly the only one. In the early days it was, if anything, more skilful. As Adrienne recalls, 'In the early days often there was no cue dot in the corner of a picture to tell you when a programme was about to end – and therefore, when you were about to broadcast. The programme would simply just suddenly end. And often with plenty of time before the next programme was to begin, so you would have to fill the time. You learnt to keep loads of material to one side for these occasions.'

But now rehearsals were over. The awaited opening night of Ulster Television had arrived and Adrienne changed into her new dress. At a quarter to five the signal from Havelock House was routed to the ITA's Black Mountain transmitter and began radiating to about 100,000 television sets. Sir Laurence opened the station with a few words and introduced the Governor, Lord Wakehurst. As the

Queen's representative, he would have ranked as the province's most elevated citizen. Adrienne faultlessly introduced herself as the announcer, digging her nails into her palms to dispel the nervousness, and went straight into forthcoming programmes. First was a live show hosted by Bea Lillie, featuring children from the streets around Havelock House indulging in Hallowe'en games now half-forgotten, like ducking for apples. (They may have been holding their breath, in case Bea was tempted to say that this was spelt with a D.) After that there followed a short tour of Northern Ireland in words and music, followed by recorded greetings from ITV stars. With that, UTV switched to network, on which was 'The Adventures of Robin Hood', the first of many successful big-budget TV shows commissioned by Lew Grade, who was later to observe wryly after the commercial failure of his feature film, *Raise the Titanic*, that it would have been cheaper to lower the Atlantic. After 'Robin Hood', the network proceeded with ITN news, '77 Sunset Strip', a Jimmy Jewel variety programme, wrestling and a Gary Cooper movie. The audience loved it all.

Meanwhile Adrienne's role was over for the day and family matters now took precedence. Her parents were holding a Hallowe'en party. Doubtless they had gathered round a screen and as far as they were concerned, the star of the evening was her – not a knighted actor, nor a noted comic actress or a high lord of the realm. The star was their own Adrienne and they were waiting for her entrance. And she felt like a star: people had sent her flowers. She was in UTV reception, waiting for a taxi, when Brum appeared, saying that he wanted to introduce her to Bea. But Adrienne wanted to get home and demurred because Bea was not in evidence. Brum insisted and eventually Bea appeared. She was a considerable celebrity in her day, honoured with a star on the Hollywood Walk of Fame and awarded a Tony award some years previously. 'I was expecting this very famous actress to tell me that with more experience, I would be fine,' says Adrienne. 'But her first words were "Darling, was I all right?" Instead she was asking me if her performance had been up to scratch. Naturally I told her that she had been wonderful. After that I went home to my proud parents, pleased with myself that I had got through it all without stumbling or crying.'

Back in the building, there were other small troubles. When the sketch with the children was ended, a telephone call came in to Havelock House asking for Mr

'School Around the Corner' was a regular in the UTV schedules for a decade from 1995. It was a window into the lives of small children, the type of programme that has become a rarity in all television of late.

MacQuitty. Bill MacQuitty was surprised because his name had not been mentioned on air. He took the call.

'You don't know me,' said a Belfast man's voice, 'but you'll rue this day's work.'

'Who are you?' MacQuitty asked.

'Never mind who I am. You know the children round the barrel?'

'No, I don't,' MacQuitty said. 'They were just ordinary children we brought in who were playing in the street outside the studio.'

'Those weren't ordinary children. They were Catholics, all of them, ye right Papist bastard.'

Bill MacQuitty realised more than ever why he did not want to be managing director once his year was up. Back in London and near the end of his promised year of service as managing director, a group of influential shareholders went to see him to urge him to remain in the post. He could name his remuneration. He told them he had other things to do.

Back that first night, Brum was dealing with Sir Laurence. The great man had been persuaded to do a reading at the end of transmission that first evening, but nobody knew what it was to be. At last, and late in the day, he told Brum it would be Addison's poem, 'The Spacious Firmament', something from Genesis and a piece from Shakespeare. This caused immediate panic. Nowhere in the station was there a Bible; nowhere in the station was there any Shakespeare. It was near shop-closing time and Brum despatched someone post-haste into the shopping centre to buy copies. A couple of rehearsals did not go well because, Brum surmised, the new staff in the new studio were nervous with the old hand Olivier. 'Clumsy and embarrassing' is how Brum described the rehearsals. Sir Laurence then retired to the sanctum of Barry Johnston's office and, with a raincoat as a headrest, lay full length on his desk. But when closedown came, as always, Laurence Olivier delivered an impeccable performance. Well, almost. Jimmy Greene had crowded into the tiny booth with Olivier in order to do the microphone switching, which the visitor would not have been familiar with. Jimmy and Olivier knew each other from touring together.

Jimmy remembers that broadcast thus: 'So he sat in the announcer's chair. I'm beside him there with my finger on the switch, and I have him switched on. He gets to where he said he was going to finish and which was "And the Lord said, let there be light, and there was . . ." and he stopped. I thought, "He's going to fall asleep. He's pissed . . . I'll switch him off!" And he said, "Light." Nobody knew that I nearly switched the Great Actor off on the first night of Ulster Television.' Later, Adrienne McGuill slipped into her bag the slip of paper upon which the Great Actor had written the running order of his epilogue.

And then it was party time in the typing pool. Adrienne left the festivities at her home and returned for the celebrations. Olivier made a speech; so did Brum. Bea Lillie and the Governor got on well; she ended up on his knee. In the circles he moved in, he might also have known her as Lady Peel. He might even have known a story about her, perhaps apocryphal, that she had once returned to her hotel a little drunk and had asked at reception for Lady's Kee's pee.

How better to celebrate the beginning of the first half-century of what Brum dubbed the 'Fun Factory' than with a good party?

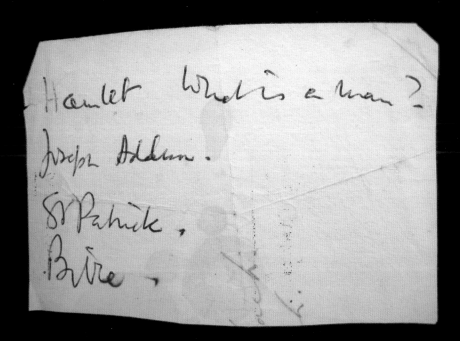

■ Sir Laurence Olivier. Sir Laurence – or Larry, as he was known to friends – gave the first epilogue at the end of broadcasting on 31 October 1959 and this is a screen-grab of that broadcast.

■ Adrienne McGuill slipped this little note into her bag at the end of the first night of UTV. It was a running order Sir Laurence Olivier wrote for himself for the epilogue at the end of UTV's first evening of programmes. It read: 'Hamlet. What is a man. Joseph Addison. St Patrick, Bible.'

Chapter 5

News to a divided audience

As we have seen, in the middle of 1959 the UTV directors were losing confidence and withdrew promises made to the ITA that they would establish a news service immediately to provide competition to the BBC news service.

The ITA was aware that Northern Ireland, with its population of roughly 1.5 million, of whom only about 100,000 had multi-channel television receivers, was easily the smallest undertaking at that time in the independent system. The Authority was therefore reluctantly willing to tolerate the lack of a news service at the beginning. UTV was obligated to provide an hour of local programming, which was to include a local news bulletin. The revised plans submitted to the ITA cut the programming down to a weekday daily 20 minutes, without any news service. The ITA Director General, in giving the go-ahead for truncated local programming, wrote that much would depend upon the imagination and ingenuity shown in giving UTV transmissions a local colour without too great an outlay. In the company's favour, the Authority also acknowledged that Ulster Television would be pioneering a regional magazine format that might serve as a model for other relatively small companies.

Notwithstanding the lack of a proper news service, within a few months UTV had made appreciable inroads into the BBC audience and was claiming two thirds of viewers. In truth, the audience was probably happy enough for the BBC to provide the news and for UTV to provide the colour – although in black and white, of course. The management had done a good job in the recruitment of their on-air personnel. Ivor Mills and Anne Gregg were relaxed in style and projected warm personalities. Jimmy Greene was a continuity announcer and doubled up doing pieces for 'Roundabout', taking over as anchor when Ivor moved over to Southern Television. One time they had a baby elephant live in the studio and Jimmy was supposed to move on cue across the studio. Except that he was unable to do so. The elephant was standing on his foot.

The programme did manage to get out of the studio, sometimes quite a long way. A good example of the imaginative approach which the ITA was demanding was the coverage of the *Canberra*. Harland and Wolff and much of the province were very proud of the *Canberra*. It was one of the biggest passenger liners constructed by the yard since the *Titanic*, and to cover the story, Adrienne McGuill reported on the latter end of its construction and covered the sea trials on the Clyde prior to the hand-over to the P&O line. It was a good editorial decision. There was immense interest in the ship, which went down the slipway on a cold, wet day only five months after the launch of UTV. The measure of public interest can be gauged by the fact that in spite of the bad weather, 11,000 people turned out to watch.

Late in the afternoon of 2 June 1961, *Canberra* set sail from Southampton on her maiden voyage, fully booked with 2,238 passengers, nearly half of them emigrants to Australia and New Zealand. On the way back, she called in at Naples, where Adrienne and her team boarded to sail the last leg back to the UK and shoot stories. The cameraman was Seán McGaffin, with Fred Corbett, editor of 'Roundabout', and Colin Lecky Thompson, first head of presentation, producing. Fred, later to join the government information service at Stormont, was also doing the sound. Television was still very new, but, as Adrienne describes, not everybody was in awe of it and not everybody would drop everything to appear:

> We arranged to interview a lady passenger for a particular time and went to
> a lot of trouble to make sure everything was just right before we called her

to the camera. For example, the illumination was not quite right so we hung sheets from the laundry to reflect light. As best we could, we set this bit of deck up like a studio. I was sent to fetch her. But I was seven minutes later than arranged because of the lighting difficulties and by the time I appeared she was about to play bridge.

'You said two o'clock,' snapped the prospective interviewee. I explained that because of the cloudy misty weather we had had to make more complicated arrangements for filming.

'No no,' retorted the woman, 'I cannot do it now. I'm playing bridge.' And with that, she shot a look across the table and said, 'Deal, dear.' I had to crawl back without her. Colin then tried to coax her but she would not budge. We had to dismantle everything and she was interviewed the next day.

But Adrienne had better luck with another female passenger, a rather heavy person, who thought that the *Canberra* deck chairs were not fit for purpose. This passenger knew about deck chairs, since she was on her fifth world cruise. In a storm off the New Zealand coast, she had fallen over while sitting in one of the chairs. Completely indifferent to what people might think, she revealed on camera that it had taken five crew members to get her back upright.

Ulster Television has outlasted the *Canberra*, which remained in service a very creditable thirty-seven years, including time as a troopship in the Falklands War. She was broken up on a beach in Pakistan in 1997.

At the outset, the resources for 'Roundabout' and other programmes were meagre, but the station did manage the beginnings of outside broadcasting. And here we mean broadcasting outside. Engineer Eric Caves recalls what was possible in those early free and easy days: 'At weekends we would take the camera on the roof if it was sunny, along with whoever was on continuity, and we linked programmes from the roof. We used the gasworks clock across the road as a station identification clock, after checking first that it was showing the correct time.'

The first real outside broadcast was shortly after UTV started. It was the day of the Lord Mayor's Show whose route took it along the Ormeau Road and past Havelock House. The weather was fine and it was too good an opportunity to miss.

On the spur of the moment, those manning the station decided to press both cumbersome UTV cameras into service. They manhandled one out into the street at the end of its long thick cable. The other they poked out of a window and in that manner covered the parade. Ernie Strathdee did the commentary on one camera and Adrienne McGuill used the other to conduct street interviews, with a microphone also on a long cable. 'These were the old Vidicon cameras,' Eric Caves explains. 'They did not have zoom lenses. Instead, the four different lenses were on a turret on the front of the camera and the cameraman had to put a hand round the front to swivel the turret for the lens he wanted. He tried to do that when the other camera was switched to air, but if that was not possible, you simply got a black frame during the change.'

The other great parade of those days was on Rag Day, the day when students from Queen's University had a licence to roam round the streets in fancy dress with collecting cans for charity, and then have a parade of floats in the afternoon. Students were expected to pull stunts. For example, I and a companion, now a pillar of the community, turned up at UTV studios in clerical garb, saying that I was a priest from Lithuania who had escaped from behind the Iron Curtain. They rumbled us immediately but I only found out when exposed live on air in the course of an embarrassing interview, which revealed, among my many knowledge gaps, that I did not even know the capital of my supposed country. The interviewer was Maurice Smyth, who was to become controller of programmes for a short while in the late eighties.

Adrienne McGuill had a more alarming rag experience: she was kidnapped by students:

> I was coming out of UTV after having signed off with the advice, 'Don't forget to turn your TV off,' and playing the national anthem. I was just about to jump into my car when I was grabbed by a number of people and bundled into another car. I was frightened until they shouted, 'It's rag, it's rag,' which calmed me down. They said they were going to hold me to ransom until UTV paid money. I thought the chances of UTV doing that were remote.
>
> They kept me overnight in a flat in Rugby Avenue. It would have been fun except that I was worried for my mother and also for my dog. The next

■ Northern Ireland Secretary of State Humphrey Atkins (*second from the left*) plays at being a train conductor when UTV sets up a temporary 'Havelock Halt' on the central line where it passed UTV. The occasion was the opening of the Holidays and Hobbies Exhibition. Also present are Mrs Margaret Atkins, Sir Myles Humphries, head of Northern Ireland Railways, and Gloria Hunniford.

day a phone call to UTV by the students established that the company had no intention of rewarding their exploit with any money. So, after parading me through Belfast on the back of a lorry I was released. I was not all that amused at the time, but looking back, I think I should simply have relaxed and enjoyed it.

Within a decade, a stunt like that could not have been envisaged as a jape, but these were relatively happy-go-lucky years.

Something of the editorial flavour of the early 'Roundabout' is illustrated in a recollection by Jimmy Greene from 1963. The actress Valerie Hobson was visiting Northern Ireland, where she had connections, as she had been born in Larne. Hobson had risen to become a prominent actress, playing Estella in David Lean's 1946 *Great Expectations*, which, incidentally, had been scripted by her first husband, Anthony Havelock-Allan. She had divorced him in the early fifties and married the Conservative minister, John Profumo, a couple of years later. Valerie did have aristocratic connections: her first husband succeeded to a baronetcy and Profumo was actually the fifth Baron Profumo, but he did not use the title. And while in Northern Ireland she was the guest of Lord Antrim, who was, of course, the Ulster Television chairman. But the background item of greatest significance was that John Profumo had just been forced out of Harold Macmillan's cabinet and out of politics altogether, because he had lied to the House of Commons about an affair with the prostitute Christine Keeler. It was a scandal of massive proportions, involving Russian spies and London high life, achieving headlines over Europe and the United States. Valerie Hobson had stood by her husband, a newsworthy aspect of the story in itself. Jimmy Greene was despatched to the Antrim household to interview her – under strict instructions not to mention or make reference in any way to the Profumo affair. The interview was about her film career. It has to be said that if the stricture had not been agreed to, Valerie Hobson would not have given an interview. She never ever spoke publicly about the scandal during her long life, which ended in 1998. Completely buried under all this was the fact that John Profumo was also one of the members of Parliament who had fought hard for the creation of independent television in the United Kingdom. He therefore had helped make UTV possible.

Valerie Hobson's connection to John Profumo meant her presence in Northern Ireland was a big news story, but it was ignored. Contrast what happened only a few years later, when Ulster Television did have a proper newsroom. The news service was introduced in November 1962. Robin Walsh was the news editor. One day Brum Henderson told him that he had been in court on a drink-driving offence and that he would rather the item did not feature in Ulster Television news bulletins. Robin told him that he was definitely going to run it, which was a brave thing to do. Brum regarded Ulster Television as his own fiefdom, and himself as editor-in-chief. Robin told the somewhat taken-aback managing director that he would run the story for three reasons. The first was that it was going to be in the news anyway, no matter what their station did. Secondly, that if Brum had been an ordinary person, then it would not be news, but since he was important, it was very definitely news. Brum quite liked that argument, but he liked Robin's third point best. 'And when we do run it tonight, Brum,' concluded Robin, 'and afterwards some of your high-placed friends approach you to have a news item they don't like taken out of our bulletins, you can tell them to fuck off.'

'Run it, run it,' beamed Brum, and departed. The item duly appeared.

But by then, Brum already knew that Robin Walsh was a bit out of the ordinary. Robin had been working in the *Belfast Telegraph* in 1964 when Fred Corbett, then in charge of 'Roundabout', gave him a call to say that he had a vacancy and he would like to meet up and have a chat with him.

'How will I know you?' asked Robin.

'I'm bald,' came the simple reply and Robin thought to himself, 'Great start.' But Fred and Robin got on well and a formal interview was arranged. At the interview, Brum postulated a big fire somewhere in Belfast, with Robin alone in the UTV newsroom. How would he deal with it? Robin launched himself. He would phone the fire brigade to ascertain the nature and seriousness of the fire, phone the police for corroboration and implications for traffic, phone the ambulance service to see if there had been any casualties, phone the – at this point Brum interrupted:

'So you wouldn't send a camera crew?'

'Another great start,' thought Robin.

But he had indeed made a favourable impression and was told immediately afterwards that he had got the job. Brum straightaway invited him up to his office for a chat. The MD threw himself into his chair in expansive mood and stuck a cigarette in his mouth. Robin pulled out his own gas lighter, leaned across Brum's desk and thumbed the wheel (lighters worked with flint in those far-off times) in front of the big man's face. Whereupon a large spike of flame erupted from the lighter, sufficient to scorch Brum's eyebrows.

'Have I still got the job?' asked Robin.

He had, partly because Brum was by now becoming accustomed to facial flaming by recruits. When Brian Waddell, one of the first producers to join UTV, who was ultimately to become controller of local programmes and a board member, was being interviewed by Brum in the very early days, Brian had also leaned forward to light Brum's cigarette with a gas lighter set too high. The managing director's eyebrows had grown back by the time Robin tackled them.

The next day, Robin joined the UTV team as a reporter – and a small team it was. Fred Corbett was at its head. He also directed the news. Not long after this time, journalists confined themselves to gathering and writing the news and television directors directed the studio cameras. The others were Jimmy Robinson, Bill McGuckian and a freelance who joined them in the afternoons, Ivan McMichael.

One day Ivan was writing the afternoon headlines. He and Brian Baird, the newsreader for many years, were friends. Baird would sit in a corner puffing his pipe and Ivan would be furiously typing the afternoon headlines. There was a football match at Windsor Park. Gordon Burns was at the match and he was detailed to give Ivan two lines for the afternoon headlines. It was about 3.30 p.m., the headlines were at 3.40 p.m. and Ivan had nothing about the match. No sign of Burns, so he phoned reception.

'Any sign of Burns yet?'

'Oh, yes. He's been in the building for five or ten minutes,' came the answer. Ivan wondered where the hell he might be. So he phoned the canteen to be told that Burns had got a cup of tea and left a couple of minutes ago. Ivan phoned around everywhere in the building he thought Burns could be. The deadline was getting ever closer and there was no sign of him. Ivan had a furious temper, and he was becoming more and more upset.

A young Brian Waddell (*far right*) showing some Playboy Bunnies the finer points of a television studio in the sixties. On the far left is Gill Henderson, cameraman.

All Brian Baird could say was, 'My boy, you'll just have to fiddle there while Burns roams.'

Ulster Television's journalism improved very considerably in the initial years. The start of a news service coincided with the provision of a new studio block, complete with film processing. Film processing was a necessity for a news service, which needed to turn around film very fast. After 'Roundabout' came more journalistic and magazine programmes – 'Newsview', 'Radius' and 'Parade'. The company was also producing 'Britain in Brief', a weekly round-up of news stories contributed by different ITV regions. In 1965 Brum Henderson was elected to the board of the news provider, ITN, to represent five of the ITV companies. The ITV companies together owned ITN.

ALLIANCE
S.D.L.P.
VAN. UN. LOY. COAL.
DEM. UN. LOY. COAL.
N. I. LABOUR
REP. CLUBS
UNIONIST
UN. W'BELFAST LOY C.
IND. UN. COAL.
LOYALIST
IND. LOYALIST
ANTI·W'P. . . . . OY.
ULSTE . . . . OY.
NAT. F. . . . . IST
INDE
LIBER
. . . D. NAT.

78 seats

Gordon Burns fronting an election programme in the early seventies on UTV. When the Troubles began, Gordon presented the nightly news programme, 'UTV Reports', covering over a four-year period events like Bloody Sunday, and the fall of the Stormont parliament in 1972.

In January 1967, 'Flashpoint', a late-evening daily current affairs programme, began: the first of its kind in Northern Ireland. It was produced by Derek Bailey, who went on to be an award-winning producer and director of note. He also in later years was to be a leading member of a group which ran against UTV for the franchise. To service 'Flashpoint', a current affairs unit was formed. UTV was by now riding high, with very healthy viewing figures. The Board reported to shareholders that the ratio of viewing in the early part of 1967 was UTV, 66 per cent, BBC, 34 per cent. In fact, Ulster Television's ratio in this two-channel world was higher than that of any other ITV region. The UK average ranged between 40 per cent and 60 per cent.

An interesting situation arose in December 1968. It was a crucial time for Northern Ireland. At Stormont, Captain Terence O'Neil was battling for his political life, trying to lead the Ulster Unionist Party, and therefore the government of Northern Ireland, down a less confrontational path. He was being opposed by sections within his own party and by Loyalists outside his party, including the Rev. Ian Paisley. The streets were filled night after night with rioters. On 9 December, O'Neil made his famous 'Ulster is at the Crossroads' speech, within which he asked, 'What kind of Ulster do you want? A happy and respected province, in good standing with the rest of the United Kingdom, or a place continually torn apart by riots and demonstrations and regarded by the rest of Britain as a political outcast?' Unfortunately, by the time the place had agreed some kind of answer, he was dead. So were a lot of other people.

This speech was pre-recorded by both UTV and BBC earlier in the day for transmission that evening. Brum Henderson was out of the province and Jim Creagh was holding the fort at UTV. The telephone rang. It was Waldo Maguire, controller of the BBC. He was in an agitated state. Somehow through a technical fault, the BBC had lost the crucial recording of O'Neil's speech. 'Could you let us have a duplicate, please?' Waldo asked an astonished Jim.

Nowadays such a speech could be dubbed onto a tape that could easily be slipped into a pocket. Or even onto a memory card. In those days however you needed a heavy, expensive cassette of 2-inch-wide tape. Jim said, 'I'll talk to our engineers and get back to you.' Jim consulted Barry Johnston and they both agreed that UTV would have to accede to the BBC request. However, Jim did talk to the engineers before phoning Waldo.

'Hello, Waldo,' said Jim. 'We're not going to give you a duplicate tape.' Jim could hear Waldo gasping audibly over the line. After a wicked little pause, he continued, 'We'll do better. We'll give you a direct feed.' In layman's language, Jim was telling Waldo that UTV would run the tape of the speech from Havelock House at the appointed time and feed by landline to Broadcasting House, thus allowing BBC to broadcast it simultaneously. Those watching the historic speech on BBC never knew that the speech was actually playing out from a UTV machine.

Recollecting the times, Jim says, 'Thereafter Waldo was almost embarrassing in the way he treated me. If we were at an event together, Waldo would greet me effusively with, "And there's my very good friend, Jim!" But he was a lovely man. He was a journalist and so was I. So any rivalry was friendly.'

Fred Corbett left UTV to join the Government Information Service and Bill McGuckian took over. Robin remembers Bill as a first-class editor, displaying both sound judgement and skill at handling people. His handling of people was put severely to the test on one occasion. Brian Durkin had been invited one afternoon into Brum's office and had partaken of much generous hospitality. This was not known to Bill McGuckian and his production team, which was unfortunate. Brian was reading the news that evening. At the top of the programme was an item about a new traffic plan for Belfast. As luck would have it, film illustrating the traffic story was joined to the programme titles, so Brian's introductory 15-second script was not in vision. It was covered by traffic pictures. Brian's piece out of vision ended, and the filmed report started immediately. However, as soon as his 15 seconds were over, Brian slumped forward in the newsreader's chair and his head hit the desk.

The floor manager in the studio, Myles Scott, leapt forward and got Brian out of the studio. This meant that when the filmed report ended, there would be nobody in the studio and the programme would come to a halt. Bill McGuckian raced from the production gallery towards the studio, intending to read the rest of the news. Again luck intervened. On his way he met Jimmy Greene coming down the stairs. Jimmy was hastily bundled into the newsreader's chair, just in time to read the rest of the news. There was a big inquest afterwards but since the managing director was implicated in what had happened, fallout was inevitably subdued.

Bill left to take charge of Royal Ulster Constabulary public relations in 1969, whereupon Robin Walsh became editor, just as the Troubles were beginning. Robin was fond of telling people afterwards that Bill had left for an easier life.

Robin was not long in the job when a little sports episode intruded into his newsman's life. The West Indies cricket team were in the United Kingdom and had agreed to play Ireland in a one-day match at the village of Sion Mills, about 75 miles from Havelock House by road in County Tyrone. In the next century the

Irish cricket team were to make their name in the West Indies, but at this time they were well down the league. The West Indies fielded a second, perhaps a third eleven team, not their top players. They even included their manager in the eleven. Robin Walsh is passionate about cricket and would have been tempted to send a reporter and crew, but to get material into that day's programme they would have had to leave after 2 or 3 hours' play to get the film back to Belfast. It was not worth it. In fact, Robin did not even bother to watch the BBC's live coverage of the game (the BBC had sent an outside broadcast unit). That afternoon Robin was in his office, monitoring the BBC's 12.55 radio news bulletin. It was a slow day with

UTV was always keen on providing programmes to bolster the business community. The series 'Headstart' in the 1980s was aimed at helping new businesses. Arnold Hatch of Craigavon featured on one of the programmes with one of his heat exchangers.

relatively uninteresting news, followed by a piece of sports news: 'And now sport. At the one-day international cricket match at Sion Mills, Ireland have bowled out the West Indies for twenty-five. Now the weather . . .' Robin shook his head in disbelief. Why wasn't this leading the BBC bulletin? What clown in the BBC had been in charge of the running order? Within minutes, Fleet Street, centre of the UK news industry, was pulling out maps to find out where Sion Mills was.

Seconds later, the phone rang at UTV. 'Ted Dutton here, Robin,' said the voice on the other end. Ted Dutton was the ITN home news editor.

'The answer's no,' Robin bellowed into the mouthpiece.

'What was I going to ask?' said Ted.

'If I have pictures of the cricket,' snapped Robin. 'And the answer's no.' For years Robin wondered what clot in the BBC had put the cricket story right at the end of the bulletin. Only years later did I tell him it was myself. I was at the beginning of my career in journalism when I wrote that news bulletin. I was told that sport went at the end of the bulletin and before the weather. I had known very little about cricket. Before the end of that day in the BBC, I knew a heck of a lot more about the game, gleaned from mocking colleagues and snorting bosses.

Ken Reid, current UTV political correspondent.

The following day, the West Indies were at the North Cricket Ground just up the road from Havelock House. 'This time, when the West Indies were batting, the ball was hardly off the Ormeau Road,' Robin says.

When the definitive history of the broadcast journalism of the Troubles is penned, the name of Robin Walsh will be one of those writ large. He played a significant part in evolving rules of engagement for broadcast journalists facing the difficulties of serving a community for which middle ground was a high plateau, steep-sided and barely attainable. The Northern Ireland upon which the Troubles descended was still old-fashioned in so many ways. It was still coming to terms with aspects of modernity, not least broadcast journalism, where the garnering of information often only just preceded its publication. In broadcasting, the act of editorship was compressed, often to the point where it could be defined as making the right choice of reporter. To illustrate, if a newsroom had a reporter at the end of a telephone witnessing a riot, and that reporter was switched straight to air to give a live report, all an editor could do was listen at the same time as the audience. For the next few seconds, that reporter was the editor of what was broadcast. This was happening in a place where within living memory, the very old-fashioned use of advertisements instead of headlines constituted the front page of the Belfast *News Letter*.

So new guidelines were needed. New ways of conveying information had to be invented, including new rules about identifying people, alive and dead, as Catholic or Protestant (and new rules about not identifying them as such); new rules about filming riots and disturbances so as not to provoke behaviour designed merely to attract television attention; new guidelines about showing faces and number plates, about interviewing paramilitary spokespersons, about back-to-camera and hooded interviews, about secret filming, about funerals and about intruding into grief, about announcing demonstrations yet to be held. In the years before 1968 and 1969, these considerations attracted little attention. Now they demanded immediate attention. The constant diet of shootings, bombings and street disorder brought with it editorial considerations unique to reporting to the very community that was tearing itself apart.

Robin Walsh was the man in charge of UTV news for the critical first five years of the Troubles. The extent to which new rules were needed was exposed in its full nakedness to Robin at a time when Belfast had erupted and the Bogside riots were at their height. The police were showing signs of not being able to contain the situation. This was August 1969, and people were fleeing over the border to escape the violence, a factor which led to an important speech by Jack Lynch on Irish television, in which he stated that the Irish government could no longer stand by. There were those in Northern Ireland who believed that this statement was hinting at military intervention by the Dublin government. Tensions were very high.

Sydney Perry, in charge of programmes at Ulster Television, argued that this statement was inflammatory and should not be carried on Ulster Television bulletins. Robin found that the lesson still had to be learnt by some in the station, that Ulster Television was not an island of news information which could be insulated: it could not use its news output for social engineering or, still worse, for supporting a government viewpoint or any other political line. Robin forcefully made the point that ignoring an important statement such as that made by Jack Lynch, already widely in the public domain, could only damage the credibility of the Ulster Television news service. Even if no other news outlet was carrying the Lynch speech, Robin's point was that the lack of responsible, accurate news would have allowed rumour to take over, with even more catastrophic results. The community had a right to know what was happening, and to know from Ulster Television. He won his point. But it was a battle needing fought several times.

During the first week of the Troubles in August 1969, ITN took the then unique decision to newscast part of the recently created 'News at Ten' live from Ulster Television's studios in Belfast. A full production team took up residence for the week and the programmes were fronted by the late Leonard Parkin. For that particular week of trouble, the top half of 'News at Ten' came from Belfast and was devoted to events in the city and the rest of the province. The rest of the news was contained after the advertising break. Then, right at the end of the bulletin, it was always back to Parkin for the latest from Belfast, almost invariably news of rioting and mayhem. This was too much for Brum Henderson. He was adamant that no mention should be made of ongoing street trouble, because it might encourage people to join the ranks of rioters. There followed a substantial row between the news people and the management of the station. The ITA regional officer for Belfast, Rex Cathcart, sided with the journalists. It eventually required the intervention of Nigel Ryan, head of ITN, who had to hop on a plane to Belfast to resolve the issue. The journalists won the day, helped by the view of Rex Cathcart. He did not think that censorship would achieve anything positive. Rex Cathcart was later to become the Professor of Education at Queen's University Belfast.

It was at a time like this that Brian Baird illustrated the black humour that became a trademark of Belfast throughout the Troubles, when he quipped, 'We interrupt this news flash to bring you an even worse one . . .'

'UTV Reports' was the focal point of the local output. It went out Monday to Friday at 6 p.m. for 33 minutes (but was often extended to fill a full hour). The programme was in full head-to-head competition with BBC Northern Ireland's 'Scene Around Six' (for which I was a reporter), and figures indicated UTV enjoyed the higher audience.

Robin Walsh extols the programme in these terms: 'Few weeks went by without two or even three of the programmes hitting the top ten at the expense of prime time programming. One of the keys to the programme's success was to be found in its presenters' robust interviewing styles – newsmakers of the day receiving little quarter from the journalistic excellence of people such as Gordon Burns and David Dunseith. The programme's on-air promotion billed it as, "UTV Reports – the programme that gets people talking."'

David Dunseith left UTV to join BBC in 1981, so this picture of a draw must have been taken on or before that date. *From left*: David Dunseith, Leslie Dawes, Lynda Jayne Stewart, Colin Baker and Derek Murray.

Among its groundbreaking items was a studio confrontation between a hooded UDA man and the MP for Foyle, John Hume, over the issue of no-go areas for the RUC and Army. It was a startling piece of television at the time, again making many headlines. (When Robin collected the UDA man, with his hood in his pocket, he said to his passenger, as they drew into the UTV car park, 'We'll pay a courtesy call to make-up – not that you'll need it.') Then there was the first discussion between Stormont and Dublin ministers during a period when Stormont broke off diplomatic relations with the South. The programme reached further. It broadcast a lengthy interview in Downing Street with Prime Minister Edward Heath, who, clearly losing his temper, described Ulster Loyalists as 'Disloyalists'. His outburst to interviewer Gordon Burns made headlines throughout the UK, and part of the interview was used by the BBC. In arranging such an interview, Robin Walsh had used UTV's editorial flexibility to the full. At

BBC Belfast, to secure an interview with the Prime Minister, the newsroom had to go through editorial layers at BBC headquarters in London. Robin simply rang ITN's political correspondent and asked him to set up an interview for Gordon Burns. Fixed!

The amount and depth of Ulster Television's news and current affairs coverage belied its small resources at the time. UTV had six journalists and three sound camera crews, at most augmented by three freelance cameramen with silent or mute cameras. What was happening on the station's doorstep was a very major story by any standards. Journalists and camera crews from other parts of the world were frequent visitors. UTV's film coverage was being used on a regular basis by television stations all over the world. In those early days, ABC of America also used the station's processing and editing facilities to feed the satellite to New York. The ABC material – like that of ITN – was made available to the local news output and it made all the difference. A small television station like Ulster Television was simply not equipped to deal with a story of such magnitude and the station could not have coped without the co-operation of ITN in particular. This network news service had virtually a full-time presence in the first few years of the Troubles. At times requiring heavy news coverage, ITN was sending over two sound crews, two reporters and a producer.

It was during these early years that young, enthusiastic ITN reporters who were later to become household names plied their trade on the streets of Belfast. Names such as Gerald Seymour, Trevor McDonald, Michael Nicholson, Michael Brunson, Peter Sissons. Gerald Seymour knew that the BBC operated a 24-hour newsroom, which UTV could not afford to do. It meant that a BBC reporter like Martin Bell could sleep knowing that if something serious happened during the night, he would be alerted. In those days, all the reporters stayed in the Europa Hotel. To make sure he was not beaten to a story, Gerald Seymour used to sleep in the foyer of the hotel. If he saw someone like Martin Bell leaving the building with a camera crew, he leapt to a phone to find out what was happening. This made sure that ITN was not scooped. Seymour was to become an internationally-respected thriller writer whose first novel, *Harry's Game*, was based on his Belfast ITN experience working out of Havelock House. *Harry's Game* was later made into a BAFTA-winning drama serial by Yorkshire Television, using a haunting theme by Clannad.

Sir Trevor McDonald, veteran ITN newscaster and a frequent professional visitor to Northern Ireland throughout UTV's history.
ITN operated out of a Portakabin on one of the flat roofs of Ulster Television, where, of all things, soft-ball cricket was played at lunchtime to relieve the pressure – with a hurley.
When Trevor McDonald was in Belfast and on the roof, he was the West Indies team.

Special mention must be made of the news camera crews, whom many reporters believe were the real heroes of the coverage. In those days, they operated under the very difficult circumstances. The cameraman was carrying a heavy 16 mm camera, usually an Arriflex. He was bound to the sound recordist by an 'umbilical cord', necessary to keep the sound film synchronised. The sound recordist carried a box slung in front, with controls for the sound. He also usually carried a spare magazine of film for the camera. As can be imagined, these two men – and they were usually men – had limited mobility because they were tethered together. While the cameraman was filming, he was blind, except to what was in his viewfinder. Mobility was therefore difficult in situations which required fleetness of foot, such as in a riot. Many a cameraman was hit over the head from behind. Good television reporters remained behind their camera crews to protect them and to act as a warning system for their blind sides.

Today's lightweight, one-person video-plus-sound news camera setup was unimaginable back then, as were instant lightweight satellite links or roadside computer editing. Those were the days of madcap dashes by road to Havelock House and an impatient 40-minute wait for the processing machine to reveal what had been taken. Then to editing, with individual shots being identified, cut out, and hung on pegs over an editing bin for assembly with transparent tape, or sometimes film cement. Leader on the front and run-out opaque film at the end. Then to telecine, ready for transmission.

The last big set piece Robin Walsh had charge of was coverage of the result of the Sunningdale talks which paved the way for the first power-sharing executive at Stormont in 1974. The talks began on a Friday night and lasted all day Saturday and into Sunday. BBC had an OB (outside broadcasting unit) at the talks and UTV

did not, which was a great advantage for the BBC. However, the talks broke up at nine in the evening, by which time ITN had managed to get an OB at the venue. Both BBC and UTV had advertised a special programme for 10 p.m. on the Sunday.

UTV's current outside broadcasting truck.

As Robin relates:

> We had David Dunseith with Derek Murray on the ground at Sunningdale. Ian Sanderson was in studio in Belfast with a group of local politicians to sustain the studio discussion, while Dunseith was getting the political leaders to the OB. I was directing the news operation and remember asking Sydney Perry and Tony Finnigan to watch BBC to see what they were doing. We mounted the programme flying by the seats of our pants. We had Edward Heath, Brian Faulkner and all the other main players except John Hume.
>
> When it was over, I asked Sydney and Tony for a rundown of the BBC's programme. I was astounded when they told me that it had not yet started. It seems a decision was made at the BBC to stick with network, because everything wasn't quite ready at the Sunningdale OB.

As it happened, the following day at ten o'clock, Robin Walsh was at the BBC to be interviewed for the post of BBC news editor at Broadcasting House. On the interviewing panel was Ronald Mason, Head of Programmes in Northern Ireland, the same Ronald Mason who, a decade before, had produced Adrienne McGuill in radio drama. His first question was: 'What did you think of our decision to postpone our special programme on Sunningdale last night and give you a free run?'

'I thought Christmas had come early,' replied Robin. He got the job, and eventually the top job as Controller of BBC Northern Ireland.

When Robin left Ulster Television, there was nothing official arranged to mark his departure. Brum Henderson would not allow any celebration or recognition of his ten exhausting, illustrious years of service, half of the period as a trailblazing editor. It was because he was going to the BBC, the rivals. But then, in another fifteen or so years, Brum himself was to exit Havelock House without ceremony – though for altogether different reasons.

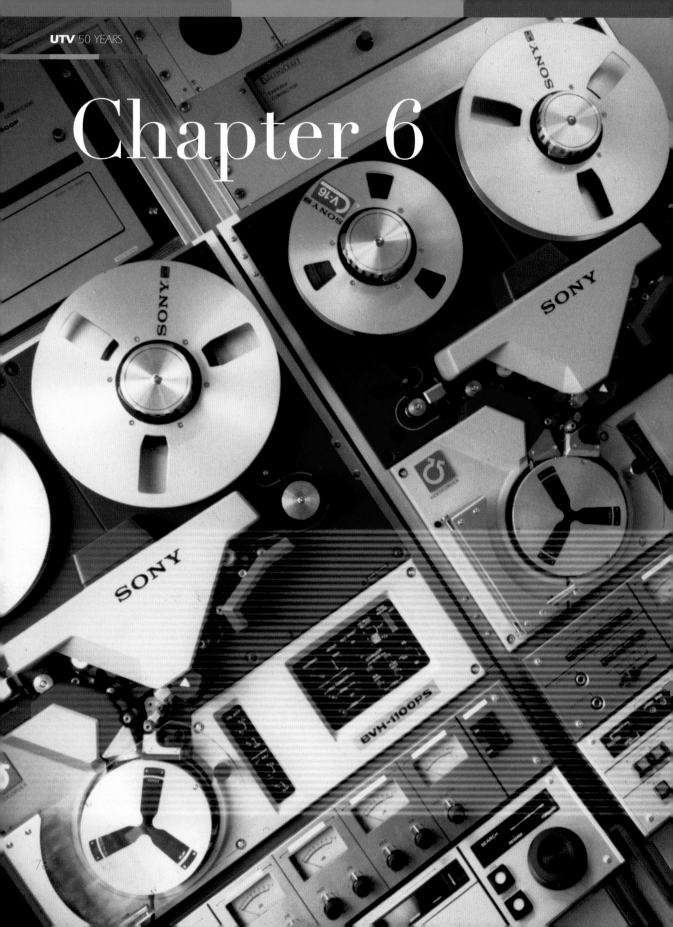

Chapter 6

A licence to print money — sometimes

Fifty years on, it is perhaps difficult to gauge the impact of advertisements on television when they first were seen by the relatively small Northern Ireland television audience in 1959. There were under 100,000 television receivers and no doubt the viewers and prospective viewers were curious, but they had been accustomed to seeing something similar at the cinema. Belfast and the towns around the province had dozens of cinemas in 1959 but most closed in the sixties and seventies as people lost the habit of cinema-going, a trend mightily reinforced by the Troubles. Some cinemas, like the Ritz (later the ABC) in Belfast's Great Victoria Street, with its famous colour-changing disappearing organ, were real palaces of delight. But many others, like the Central Cinema in Belfast's Smithfield area, were far from plush, as made plain by common nicknames of 'The Bughouse' and 'The Fleapit'. The cinema as an entertainment would not recover in the public's affection until recent times.

However, if audience expectations of moving-image advertisements in the middle of the last century were based on their cinema experiences, then they would have been low. Forget the glossy, high-impact surround sound computer-enhanced cinema advertisements of today. In the decade following World War II, cinema advertisements seem to have been limp, half-hearted efforts. Cinema as an advertising medium experienced a continual decline in the percentage of total advertising expenditure, falling from 4 per cent in 1948 to 1 per cent in 1960. A report published by the Institute of Economic Affairs in 1966, not all that long after UTV had begun transmissions, contained the following observation about cinema advertising: 'Another audience grievance concerns advertisement films. A great many of these are inept and cheap-jack snippets of poor quality which a national television contractor would be ashamed to transmit . . .'

The greatest difference with respect to advertising between cinema and television was that such income was icing on the cake for cinema. For independent television, advertising was lifeblood.

That would have been known to Basil Lapworth, UTV's first advertising manager. His background was in Belfast cinema management. He had been in charge of the fortunes of the Hippodrome (later the Odeon and then the New Vic) next door to the Belfast Royal Opera House (which was also a cinema at that time). Before that, Basil had been manager of the Royal cinema in Arthur Street, Belfast. Nor would screen advertising have been in any way strange to Stanley Wylie, who became one of UTV's first transmission controllers in 1959. Wylie was a musician and had succeeded the great Joseph Seal as organist at the Ritz cinema. When it came to recruitment to the new station, the perceived shared attributes of the two businesses were too obvious to ignore. In 1959, there was no pool of television talent to draw upon, at least not in Northern Ireland. In fact, there weren't many television professionals in the whole of Europe, never mind Ireland. RTÉ did not begin until 1961.

David Lyle, chief executive of a leading Northern Ireland advertising agency, LyleBailie International, remembers his first experience of doing business with UTV in 1975, as a young employee of Armstrong Long Advertising. Roland Long was very friendly with the UTV sales director, Mike Hutcheson. He told the new recruit that he should meet Basil, and David was duly sent to UTV for a morning

A housewife in Newry walked into a grocers, ordered three types of cheese, pickles from Poland, a bottle of Burgundy

...and nobody stared!

Nobody in the shop thought it unusual when she bought these delicacies and deposited them in the back seat of her Mini. Later she and her husband enjoyed a few glasses of Pommard with the beautifully ripe Camembert.

Smartly dressed young housewives in their own cars with well filled purses are just as common in Ulster as anywhere in Britain. You'll find them in Newry, Ballymoney, Enniskillen, Belfast – all over Northern Ireland.

Mrs. Average Northern Ireland Housewife actually controls a greater volume of spending power than her sister on the mainland.

But don't get the wrong impression. The young housewife isn't always shopping. Most evenings she just stays at home and watches Television. She watches Ulster Television and those advertisements for cheeses, pickles and bottles of wine, as well as for other contemporary delicacies like Marvel Instant Non-Fat Milk, Lyons Ready Brek, Birds Dream Topping and Yeoman Instant Mashed Potatoes.

 Ulster Television

UTV advertising itself in the late sixties. The message is that Newry housewives were as sophisticated as any in their shopping, but did not shop in the evenings. That was when they watched UTV and its advertisements, of course.

There was a piece of rope in Newry with a farmer on one end and a pig on the other and as they walked up the High Street

...everyone stared!

The pig too was surprised – rather embarrassed in fact. He had seen his sty mates being taken off in a trailer drawn by a new Rover 2000.

People living in towns in present day Ulster are accustomed to a prosperous modern minded farmer. The sort of man who has central heating in his house, whose shirt is whiter than white, who likes a Dry Martini before lunch and a good cigar after dinner. The sort of man whose wife wouldn't dream of letting him bring home the bacon unless it was nicely wrapped in cellophane and had been bought at Liptons, British Home Stores, Spar or Home & Colonial.

Northern Ireland is the U.K's. foremost growth market – a market that is mainly urban and industrial but with a strong prosperous agricultural section. A market that is easily reached through Ulster Television.

 Ulster Television

UTV advertising itself in the late sixties. Counterpart to the 'Nobody Stared' Newry advertisement. Whether the line about the Ulster farmer with his Martini before lunch and good cigar after dinner was believable anywhere, including Newry, is debatable.

Ever opportunistic, UTV reminded advertisers in the sixties of the drawing power of Wimbledon tennis on television. The punster copywriter was enjoying him- or herself.

meeting in Basil's office. 'A larger than life character,' says David. 'First there was coffee, then out came the brandy bottle and the coffee was topped up with that.'

Television advertising did not begin in the United Kingdom until ITV began in September 1955, a mere four years before UTV came on air. The first advertisement on that first commercial TV station in London was for Gibbs SR toothpaste, as the setters of pub quizzes will already know. A tube of toothpaste was depicted in a block of ice to suggest tingling freshness with such impact, the copywriters must have been hoping, that the audience would forget that toothpaste stuck in a block of ice is useless and that in those frigid circumstances, the handbasin taps would probably have been frozen as well.

Bernard Levin was a foremost and very acerbic newspaper columnist writing for the *Guardian*, which was the *Manchester Guardian* at the time. He was the man who, in a more respectful age, once wrote of the Conservative Attorney General, Sir Reginald Manningham-Buller, as Sir Reginald 'Bullying Manner'. Levin was aware that those opposed to commercial television feared the americanisation of the British way of life. Television advertisements, it was being asserted, would undermine cherished, age-old values. Bernard Levin wrote the day following that first evening of commercials: 'I feel neither depraved nor uplifted by what I have seen . . . Certainly the advertising has been entirely innocuous. I have already forgotten the name of the toothpaste.' He had yet to learn, if he ever did, that one of the means by which broadcast advertising succeeds is through repetition. The viewer might very well forget a product name on first broadcast, but not so easily after twenty or more repetitions.

Since British cinema seemed to have little in the way of expertise to offer advertising copywriters for this new television medium, it was natural, notwithstanding the critics of the system, for attention to turn to the other side of the Atlantic for guidance: to Madison Avenue in New York. Commercial television had blossomed in the United States after World War II, so the advertisement makers drew upon the American experience. It was all there was. But there were drawbacks. American television tended to use live commercials, sponsored programs, and filmed commercials of 60 seconds rather than the 7 to 30 seconds usual in Britain, where, additionally, sponsored programmes were forbidden by the ITA. Nowadays, British advertising airtime is sold in multiples of 10 seconds, and the most popular time length is 30 seconds. There were other important differences relating to culture and lifestyle, which in those early days provoked the head of one prominent London advertising agency to castigate American advertisers as 'loud-mouthed salesmen who confused shouting with communicating and bullying with persuading'. British advertising as it developed into the sixties and seventies tended to be less detailed and more soft-sell. John Crosby, the noted American syndicated television critic who wrote many years for the *New York Herald Tribune*, commented on British television advertisements in the following terms: 'They were – I'm forced to confess – fearfully British and frightfully uninsistent. One of them opened with a hearty Briton saying, "Hello there. I want to talk about penguins." And talk about penguins he did – about small penguins that live off the coast of Africa, about King penguins who warm their eggs between their feet and about imperial penguins. "And also the other kind of penguin," he concluded diffidently, "milk chocolate Penguins," and he held up a bar. "Biggest milk chocolate bar in Britain."' The American audience would never have understood that piece of copywriting, and, I am tempted to add, neither would a British or Irish television audience today. However, it is well to remember that television advertisements were snapshots of the fashions of their times.

So the advent of UTV coincided with the British advertising industry discovering its own methodology and comfort zones. Some of the first attempts became famous for getting it very badly wrong. One of the most notable advertising blunders was the campaign for Strand cigarettes in UTV's second year. The viewers loved the advertisement, which showed a dark, damp street of shadows and pools of light in a city like London, occupied by a lone figure looking a little like a young Frank Sinatra, replete in a trenchcoat with a black felt trilby hat tilted back on his head. The man lit his Strand cigarette and the voiceover said, 'You're never alone with a Strand.' With that, the music played and the man walked slowly off – alone. The advertisement itself was a hit. Viewers wrote in to the television companies asking for the music, so the composer, Cliff Adams, hurriedly expanded the jingle into 'The Lonely Man Theme' instrumental, which achieved a modicum of success in the UK singles chart. However, the public began associating Strand cigarettes with bleakness and loneliness, and avoided them. The Wills tobacco company withdrew the brand in the early sixties and the advertisements became infamous as an object lesson in how not to advertise. Cigarette advertising was banned from television in 1965.

But in the beginning, UTV would have taken any advertising it could grab, be it good, bad or indifferent. As the network of ITV companies was extending broadly northwards in the UK, the attention of media buyers – the people who place advertisements in television and other media – was directed at the stations which were serving the areas of greatest population. These would have been London, the Midlands, the conurbations of England. An advertisement on the TV

station serving the midlands of England would be transmitted to a population of 20 million people. Northern Ireland had a population of around 1.5 million, a significant part of which could not receive television before the transmitters outside Belfast were built.

Paul Hutchinson, UTV's current sales director Ireland, explains: 'The difficulty we had in the early days was that UTV was not deemed to be a must-have ITV television region.' When UTV came on air, there was already a history of buying in the existing bigger TV companies. In the rankings of television companies, UTV was a tiddler and it is fair to say that in the big smoke of London, Northern Ireland, with a population the equivalent of about four London boroughs, was out of sight and out of mind. Big advertisers such as Procter & Gamble and Unilever knew about UTV, but a lot of the other advertising professionals did not.

Other difficulties existed for the new company. Advertisers are a hard-headed bunch, and no matter how much a majority in Northern Ireland might declare itself as British as Yorkshire, the advertising fraternity knew it was not. Take new car registrations, for example. In the rest of the UK the registration plates had letters denoting the year of registration, which incongruously started on 1 August. In Northern Ireland, it was 1 January and the number plates did not have obvious dating. Motor dealers in Great Britain knew there would be a surge in new car sales just after the year change in August, except in Northern Ireland, and consequently would leave Northern Ireland and UTV out of the national vehicle advertising spree. (The dating elements of car registrations have since changed.)

Furthermore, Northern Ireland had a unique retail structure, particularly with respect to supermarkets. The UK multiples of Sainsbury's and Tesco did not exist in Ireland. In the early years, the big names in Northern Ireland grocery retail were Stewarts, out ahead of all others, followed by Wellworths, Crazy Prices, Mace, Spar, VG and the Co-op. Independent grocers had almost a quarter of the market. But the big media buyers across the water were accustomed to advertising Sainsbury's and Tesco and later Asda throughout the rest of the UK. Again, UTV lost out, because Tesco and Sainsbury's did not arrive in NI until around 1997, Asda in 2005. Then there was the banking structure. Northern Ireland had names like the Belfast Banking Company, the Northern, the Ulster, the AIB (which became First Trust), the Bank of Ireland. These were not high street banking names in the rest of the UK, names the media buyers associated with big advertising budgets and big markets. So UTV was largely left out by that sector.

Another difference lay in own-label selling. Some will remember the Yellow Pack budget generic groceries in Stewarts and other stores in Ireland. They were modestly successful. However, during the sixties, seventies and eighties, when supermarkets in the rest of the UK were moving into own label, Northern Ireland remained very much wedded to buying familiar branded goods, which, as Paul Hutchinson observes, 'is why the Procter and Gambles, Unilevers and Kelloggs have always supported Ulster Television well'.

Tony Axon, now with the Navigator Blue advertising agency in Belfast, began his association with television advertising in the sales department of UTV in its early days. He remembers the impact which access to television advertising made upon local advertisers: 'Advertising in those days was showbiz. When clients became involved they loved rubbing shoulders with people who were household names. There was glamour, fun and fame for the client and a tour of Ulster Television, terminating in glasses of whiskey in Basil Lapworth's office. Brum ensured that UTV was a very welcoming company.' However, it still took time for local advertisers to realise what they could do, according to Axon: 'Most of the local advertisers did not realise they could be on television. They seemed to have a mental block, thinking it would be too expensive to be advertising alongside some of the biggest names in business. But others, like Christie's Wallpapers, were hooked on their advertisements. William Christie was Lord Mayor of Belfast and I used to visit the Mayor's Parlour and talk advertising over china cups of coffee.'

There was a yarn circulating in Belfast around this time. Joe Cairns and William Christie were rivals in Belfast City Council, where both had achieved mayoral office. Joe Cairns was also in retail, selling, among other things, fireplaces. When he achieved a knighthood, someone proposed an advertising slogan for him: 'For a night by the fire, why not have a fire by the knight?'

Tony Axon, media director of Navigator Blue advertising agency.

Local advertisers were important, but it was vital for UTV to attract advertisers from across the water because that was where the really big advertising budgets lay. Perhaps twice a month a group of big advertisers would be flown over to UTV, do a little business at Havelock House and then be taken off to Royal County Down for a game on one of the world's great golf courses, followed by dinner. As Sir Thomas Lipton, one-time member of the Royal Ulster Yacht Club and tea baron of another age, neatly put it: 'There's no fun like work.'

It was plain to UTV that the London market needed a more detailed and technical education about the opportunities, so early in its life UTV began its series of marketing guides to Northern Ireland. These publications set out basic facts about the province for advertising agencies in London. As a picture of life as it was, they make interesting reading today. Take, for example, the marketing guide issued in 1989. It forecast that with Northern Ireland's rate of natural increase in population (standing at 7.6 per 1,000, as against 2.4 in the United Kingdom as a whole!), the population of Northern Ireland in 2001 would be 1,681,000. The 2001 recorded census figure was 1,685,267. It was an astoundingly accurate prophecy – a mere 4,267 out. Not a bad piece of work by the Northern Ireland Registrar General's office, accredited with this projection.

Under the heading of income and expenditure, that same 1989 guide said the following:

> Although the average income in Northern Ireland falls short of the national average, it is expenditure in the form of disposable income which is a more significant indicator from a marketing point of view. In this context, the much lower housing costs in Northern Ireland mean that households can retain a much larger proportion of their money for items other than mortgage or rates.
>
> Average house prices in Northern Ireland are much lower than the national average: in the latest Halifax Building Society index, 55% of the national level. As an example of comparative prices, a typical 4 bed-roomed detached house will fetch a price of £55,000 in Northern Ireland, compared with perhaps three or four times that level in many parts of Britain.

That 1989 guide did not forecast that, partly due to the influence of the Celtic Tiger economy driving up prices from south of the border, a decade and more later, house prices in Northern Ireland would rocket to match those of the most expensive parts of the UK – until recession took hold, of course.

In its comment on the car market, the report said: 'Northern Ireland has a very high proportion (6.3%) of the United Kingdom's surfaced roads, a feature which not only makes motoring a much less stressful experience, but almost certainly contributes to the appreciably higher annual mileage (10,400), compared with the United Kingdom average of 8,700 miles.'

Slight touch of the rose-coloured spectacles in this observation. The high road mileage may have had something to do with the fact that the Ulster Transport Authority closed down about 60 per cent of Northern Ireland's railway network, throwing traffic growth onto the roads. Furthermore, since the Troubles were continuing, many town centres were blocked to traffic as a security measure and police and Army checkpoints, static and migratory, were a feature of the landscape. All this would have been apparent to the UK television audience, including media buyers, from a couple of decades of news coverage of the violence. The description of Northern Ireland motoring being much less stressful might have drawn a few wry smiles.

However, setting aside the Troubles, the factors that made Ulster Television and its transmission area different could be turned to advantage. You have only to look at a map to see Northern Ireland's physical separation from the rest of the UK. The place could almost be considered an island, if you viewed the border as having some of the delineating attributes of a coastline. So UTV sold Northern Ireland as a great place to test a market. A test market can be a geographic region used to gauge the viability of a product or service in the mass market, before committing to full-scale marketing and selling. To find a test market region for a client, an advertiser would be looking for a population that is sufficiently similar to the eventual market in mind and relatively isolated from densely populated media markets, so that advertising to the test audience can be efficient and economical. Northern Ireland fitted that bill quite well. Almost uniquely, UTV's television area did not overlap with that of any other ITV company. Furthermore, although the marketing guides trumpeted the dominance of UTV as an advertising medium, they were not narrow in their focus. They also gave audience figures for commercial radio and circulation figures for the *Belfast Telegraph*, *Sunday World*, *News Letter* and *Sunday Life* newspapers, as well as listing about sixty local newspapers and free sheets.

UTV's 6th marketing guide, written in 1984. Many data marketing sources omitted Northern Ireland at the time. These guides therefore plugged that gap.

89

MONDAY 20ᵗ NOVEMBER, 1967   THE TIMES MONDAY

Take a trip through the UK's foremost growth market

Touch down at Aldergrove Airport, just 2 hours from London's West End... Drive

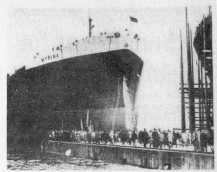

into Belfast and look round the shipyards where Europe's largest tankers are built . . . .

. . .drive out the new motorway to Coleraine and inspect the new University of Ulster. . .

Advertising in the *London Times* in 1967. It encapsulates a mood of optimism in some sections of the population just before the 30 years of mayhem broke out. I wonder if anyone ever tried to find that new motorway to Coleraine. They still wouldn't find it!

UTV knew that test marketers would probably want to use those outlets as well for their advertising. The guides listed Northern Ireland distribution companies, market research companies and consultants and over a dozen advertising agencies. The stratagem was reasonably successful. Companies using Northern Ireland to test products included household names like Cadbury, Procter and Gamble, Lever Brothers and Kraft.

And finally, Ulster Television actually advertised itself and Northern Ireland by buying airtime on English television stations in the sixties. It was an unusual if not unique step for one ITV television company to advertise on another, other than through programme promotion. Frank Carson was the voice and the scripts homed in on the clichés that Northern Ireland suffered from. For example, the images in the commercials might show a run-down area with the strapline: 'This is not Northern Ireland. It is northern England.' Or show something sophisticated with the line: 'This is not Richmond. It is Northern Ireland.' Some years later, such advertising would not be needed. The television audience in Great Britain and elsewhere would have Northern Ireland on their television screens nearly every week, eradicating any possible confusion with northern England, still less Richmond.

In 1992 Ulster Television made a major change in the way it marketed itself to the big media buyers, when it decided to end its own sales operation in London and hand over to a sales house called TSMS – Television Sales and Marketing Services. This had the effect of making UTV part of a larger selling group, comprising the television companies of Central and Anglia, whose audiences were very much larger than those of UTV. Central, based in Birmingham, had about a 15 per cent share of total ITV homes, Anglia, based in Norwich, had about 6.5 per cent and UTV, 2.3 per cent, so together the grouping constituted approximately a quarter of the homes of the whole system. As Paul Hutchinson explains, 'It meant that when agencies were having conversations about their advertising activity, UTV was at the same meeting that Central and Anglia were at. This bumped us up the list quite a bit and led to a significant increase in the UTV share of total ITV revenue. We went from something like 1.46 per cent to two per cent during the period that ITV was growing. It might look like a small increase, but for UTV income, it meant a lot.'

It was around this time that UTV began turning its attention to the Dublin market. During the late eighties the UTV signal had gone out on cable in the Republic, where at the time there was no other means of getting a popular programme like 'Coronation Street'. UTV's signal was being received in over 90 per cent of homes in Dublin. Advertisers were becoming aware of this large audience for UTV south of the border, which meant that UTV's total audience was bigger than was being reported by the Northern Ireland audience research panel. For every viewer an advertiser bought in the north, he or she got one viewer free in the south. Yet, while Brum Henderson was at the helm, there was no attempt to sell UTV airtime in Dublin. He believed that there was a gentleman's agreement between RTÉ and UTV not to do so. However, with the advent of new television stations and the consequent increased competition for revenue, this hazy informal agreement evaporated.

UTV was picking up advertising revenue from Dublin, but the Dublin business was being run by Paul Hutchinson in Belfast. Not ideal, so he brought TSMS people to Dublin to survey the possibilities. The result was the setting up of a four-person TSMS office in Dublin to service this business and to talk to the advertising agencies there. This aroused the interest of what is known in the trade as the FMCG group – Fast Moving Consumer Goods, companies selling groceries and companies like Diageo (which includes Guinness and is possibly the largest multinational drinks company in the world). The Dublin office made these companies aware that not only was the UTV signal in Dublin through cable, it was also getting to Cork, Limerick and Galway. Since the majority of the population of Ireland lives in conurbations, this knowledge made UTV more attractive than its share of homes in the UK indicated.

But it was not all plain sailing when it came to selling advertising on an all-Ireland basis. To be fully effective, an advertiser needed to be selling the same product or service north and south. It suited the makers of Mars, but it did not suit the banks because the currencies were different and so were the interest rates. It did not suit some businesses based in both parts of Ireland, such as Dunnes Stores, because the cost of beans in the two stores was different. But considering the whole island as a single market worked for more categories than not, with the result that a lot of advertisers moved their business out of the London market into the Irish market and employed an advertising agency in Ireland, mostly in Dublin. This was a very good development as far as UTV was concerned.

At the outset UTV took around 70 per cent of its revenue from the London market and 30 per cent from the home market of Northern Ireland and later the Republic. Today UTV is spreading its revenue source between Great Britain and Ireland more evenly – 52 per cent from both parts of Ireland and 48 per cent from London. This is much more to its liking. There is even a compensating mechanism between Belfast and Dublin because when one is depressed the other can be buoyed up. Altogether, this is better than for a company such as Central in central England, which derives about 94 per cent of its revenue from London.

The other side of the advertising business which UTV was not directly involved in was the making of advertisements, although for a short period in the eighties, UTV did own a percentage of a company called HETV, which made commercials. But the making of commercials, good commercials, was as vital to the health of UTV as it was to the whole ITV system.

In the fifties, many advertisements were live, read over 7-second slide pictures by the announcers. In the early days of television, there

UTV advertising itself in the late sixties, making the point that Ulster fridges were filled with the same foodstuffs as counterparts elsewhere and that advertisers should recognise the fact.

was no means of pre-recording material other than on film, which would have made 7-second advertisements too expensive. After an initial period of very basic and simple advertisements, the seventies ushered in more sophisticated slide advertisements with pre-recorded voiceovers. For even more sophistication, advertisers could also have a music soundtrack, allowing slides to become more attractive to client and viewer alike. A big retail advertisement would be filmed in UTV studios and UTV studio directors like Andy Crockart also directed commercials.

David Lyle learnt his craft writing 7-second slide commercials, mastering the skill of condensing the message. He describes writing advertisements thus:

> The UTV seven-seconders were a great discipline. Advertising trains you in précis. Quite a number of literary writers were at one time advertising copywriters. I listened to Salman Rushdie speaking at an IAPI (Institute of Advertising Practitioners in Ireland) Advertising Effectiveness Award function in Dublin. He talked in great detail about his life as an advertising copywriter. Copywriting sustained him while he was trying to build his life as an author.
>
> In advertising writing you need to listen to people on buses and trains, to real dialogue. This informs whatever kind of writing you are doing, including advertising. In advertising writing you need to combine both linear and lateral thinking skills. You need to have enough fascination for detail to think logically through the situation. You need to enjoy working out what is unique, essential and different about a product – what makes it special. That is a logical process. We can say the product is brighter, sweeter, tastier, but logically what people are interested in is the element that is warm and appealing. You want an emotional response from the viewers.

Around the time UTV began, advertising was dominated by the concept of the unique selling proposition, which is a very rationalist idea. It is an American concept dating from the forties which supposes that an advertiser can isolate something that is unique to a particular product, something which swings opinion. Partly as a reaction against concentration on USP, creative copywriters wanted to do more. They wanted to make advertising more interesting and more entertaining. They wanted to use imagination to turn a unique selling proposition into a unique *story* proposition, which would do the selling. It did not always work, as the Wills tobacco company found out with their beautifully made, atmospheric Strand story of loneliness.

But in those early days, you made the advertisement and found out whether it worked when it was exposed to public scrutiny. If it worked, fine; if not, the advertiser had wasted money. Tony Axon remembers Rex McKane, a legendary figure in the Belfast advertising world, sketching out an idea for an advertisement in his presence. Axon was amazed to see that advertisement on air six weeks later. That does not happen today.

David Lyle of the LyleBailie advertising agency in Belfast.

John Wanamaker, who died in 1922, pioneered the idea of the department store and changed the shopping experience of his hometown of Philadelphia and later the world in the late 1800s. He invented the price tag, opened the first in-store restaurant and printed the first copyrighted store advertisement. Wanamaker was a religious man who believed very much in emphatically truthful advertising. He would not have liked today's commercial television because he was strongly opposed to advertising on a Sunday. So we can assume he was being very honest when he declared, 'Half the money I spend on advertising is wasted. The trouble is I don't know which half.' As the former executive editor of the Harvard Business Review, Nicholas Carr, asserted, 'Advertising and promotion have always been frustratingly imprecise.'

Notwithstanding Carr's view, today there are more tools available for assessing advertising impact. Making a modern advertisement can be very expensive, which is why many clients now go for pre-testing of ideas before committing themselves. The best way to do this is to produce initially two or three ideas for testing. Advertising agencies learn from experience what ideas tend to work, but it is far better to spend £20,000 at the pre-testing stage than £250,000 on a production that might not work. 'We are lucky in that we work with clients who want to pre-test,' says David Lyle. 'If it is public money, it dare not be wasted. We believe passionately in psychological pre-testing. We are not so keen on the old way of relying on a single source of research, such as the focus groups. We use them alongside other techniques.'

It is at this point that the world of advertising crosses in an odd way with the world of the 'Who Wants to be a Millionaire?' television quiz show. The American essayist and journalist, HL Mencken, who died in 1956, famously wrote: 'No one in this world, so far as I know, has ever lost money by underestimating the intelligence of the great masses of the plain people.' Against that observation is the theory of the wisdom of crowds, which is based on a story, again from the late 1800s, about the scientist and statistician, Francis Galton, who was surprised when he analysed the results at a country fair when a crowd was asked to guess the butchered weight of an ox. When individual guesses were averaged, that number was much closer to the ox's butchered weight than the estimates of any individual in the crowd and, more surprisingly, also closer than any of the estimates made by cattle experts. From this was constructed the theory of the wisdom of crowds.

This theory lies behind some advertising research. If a diverse group of individuals, who are independent of each other, are asked to guess the correct answer to something, they will quite often get the right answer, or closer to the right answer than one or two experts. That is why on the quiz programme 'Who Wants to be a Millionaire?', asking the audience is a good strategy for contestants. The wisdom of crowds theory kicks in, so that the crowd making up the studio audience get it right more often than the friends who are phoned, who might nevertheless be experts.

Having said that, there are many among UTV's audience in Northern Ireland, including myself, who have witnessed at uncomfortably close quarters the

With David Dunseith is Paul Smith, architect of the celebrated quiz show 'Who Wants to be a Millionaire'. He worked at the beginning of his career at UTV. He began Celador in London, where he came up with the 'Millionaire' format. Smith is chairman and joint managing director of Celador Films, whose most famous credit is *Slumdog Millionaire*.

madness of mobs, crowds within which there was no shard of wisdom. To which David Lyle replies, 'If you corrupt the wisdom of crowds by departing from independence and diversity in the selection of the crowd make-up, if you introduce social network linkages or anything that feeds a herd instinct, then the wisdom of the crowd collapses. TV works best when appealing to the wisdom of crowds rather to the base instincts of the herd.'

The famous anti-terror advertisements of the late eighties were an attempt to modify base instincts. These award-winning advertisements broke new ground in broadcast advertising, but were almost forbidden. A reminder of what they contained. Julie-Anne Bailie, now executive creative director of LyleBailie, wrote the scripts. For one of the last of them and maybe the best-remembered one, her inspiration was a scene in a UTV documentary which showed a small girl with a lunch box under her arm outside Crumlin Road Prison in Belfast, waiting to enter for a visit. (Perhaps to her father.) That scene provoked a train of thought out of which emerged a storyline about the son growing up to be just like his father, a terrorist. It was a bleakly emotional message about the terrible cycle that needed to be broken. This advertisement was also notable for using 'Cat's in the Cradle', the 1974 folk rock song by Harry Chapin, which set to music a poem by Chapin's wife, telling the story of a father who is too preoccupied to spend time with his son. The final lines are: '*And as I hung up the phone, it occurred to me/He'd grown up just like me/My boy was just like me . . .*'

The advertisements were commissioned by the Northern Ireland Office, and their impact was very powerful. At the outset, the problem was that in the UK, political advertising on broadcast media is forbidden.

There was an undoubted political element to these advertisements, as Andy Wood, who was Director of Information at the Northern Ireland Office (NIO) from 1987 to 1997, makes clear:

> The genesis of the advertisement was the following. Tom King, Secretary of State for Northern Ireland, wanted to publicise a new, single confidential phone number and thought at the same time it would be a 'tremendous idea' to get the BBC to make a film showing the valuable work done by the security forces. He was gung-ho and had no concept of editorial independence. With a sinking heart and knowing fine what the answer would be, I approached the BBC Northern Ireland controller and in due course got the expected rejection. Faced with this, King had to accept that the only way he could get a Government-approved version on air was to make a commercial and pay for it to be screened. The first advertisement, which publicised the telephone number, went through all the approval stages and air time was booked and paid for, starting on a Monday evening.
>
> The previous week I had been a guest at an IBA dinner. Tony Fleck, the IBA officer in Belfast, asked if I would have a private word with John Whitney, the director General of the IBA. Whitney suggested firmly but politely that the launch of the first advertisement be put off because the timing was not right.

Andy Wood replied that at this late stage he had no intention of pulling the advertisement. The real reason for the confrontation was that the IBA was having cold feet. It was beginning to think that the advertisements could be challenged as being political. However, the NIO pushed ahead with what became an internationally acknowledged series of groundbreaking advertisements, and nothing more was heard of this matter.

But the golden age of local advertising may be behind us. In fact, if what Tony Axon says comes to pass, then the days of local advertising on television may be ending soon. The culprit will be the onset of the digital age. Northern Ireland will be the last area in the United Kingdom to have its analogue television signal switched off, an event scheduled for 2012. Analogue is the way television has normally been received since UTV began. When homes in Northern Ireland are forced to go digital, they will enter an arena with a very large number of available channels. According to Axon, when that happens, experience in other areas shows that viewing of traditional channels is cut in half:

> There will come the point when logically it does not make sense for me to invest in advertisement production just for that smaller size of audience. The key is the percentage of a client's total spend. At the moment, the production of an advertisement is probably about fifty per cent of spend. If production is, say, ten thousand pounds and the client's budget is twenty thousand pounds – fine. But if the client can only spend fifteen thousand pounds and his advertisement production cost remains the same at ten thousand pounds, clients might begin to think that they are spending too much money on production and not enough on reaching people. It might be better to use radio, print or posters or whatever. I'm warning clients now that they cannot be TV dependent any longer.

Tony Axon believes that this scenario could be with us within five years of going digital. There may be some inside UTV who have been gazing into the same crystal ball.

Chapter 7

Gloria and UTV

Gloria Hunniford attended the same school as I did in Portadown in the fifties. We fellow pupils did not suspect that she would become a nationally known big name so soon. In those days famous people were older people, except game players and other athletes, none of who had become rich through celebrity.

Bill Haley's song, 'Shake, Rattle and Roll' had emerged as a hit in the mid-fifties and the release of that single is often described as a demarcation line between the age of rock and what had gone before. But it was a delineator in more ways. Haley was in his thirty-first year when 'Shake, Rattle and Roll' hit the streets. By contrast, Elvis Presley released 'Heartbreak Hotel', 'Blue Suede Shoes', 'Tutti Frutti', 'Love Me Tender' and a cover of 'Shake, Rattle and Roll' in 1956, when he was only twenty-one. Cliff Richard, to become a friend of Gloria's later, released 'Travelin' Light' and 'Living Doll' in 1959, at the age of nineteen. After 'Shake, Rattle and

Portadown College was co-educational and, unusually at the time, held what would be now called a disco at lunchtime in the multipurpose gym hall. This was a development from earlier dance classes, which Gloria recalls in her book, *Gloria*: 'Every lunch hour I would tear home on my bike, gulp down my poor mother's lovingly prepared pies and tarts, then it was off back to school again to catch the half hour or so left of ballroom dancing classes.' Gloria was talking about the samba, foxtrot, tango and the waltz, which belong to that pre-'Shake, Rattle and Roll' era. Because there was no television to speak of, the school staff might not have known that in the United States, television networks had banned shots of 'Elvis the Pelvis' from the waist down because of his pelvic thrusts in time to the beat, so they had no objection to pupils bringing in their own Elvis 78s to be played on the school gramophone through biggish speakers. Occasionally the splendid headmaster, Donald Woodman, who ran the college with a nod in the direction of a minor English public school, would walk among the lunchtime dancers to instil some propriety. If the song was 'Shake, Rattle and Roll', then it was new-fangled jiving he worried about. Some of the girls forgot to keep one arm down to prevent their gymslips spinning out to display regulation blue school knickers. He would stop that. And if the song was 'Love Me Tender', some of the senior couples danced too close for his comfort. He stopped that too. But most times, it was free and easy and, truthfully, it was largely girls dancing with girls because many boys were too shy to ask a girl to dance.

Gloria was removed from the school at the age of fifteen by her father to be sent to a technical school, in spite of protests from Gloria herself and, more strenuously, from headmaster Woodman. He took the unusual step of cycling – he cycled everywhere, long before the word 'green' was applied to anything other than grass and hills – to the Hunniford home to plead for an academic career for the girl. To no avail. Mr Hunniford sincerely believed that his daughter would have a better start in life if she learnt some vocational and commercial skills at Portadown Technical College, like shorthand and typing. But Gloria's father managed to lay the foundations of her career. It was a spin-off from his conjuring with the Mid Ulster Variety Group, which toured local schools, church halls and community halls. Before television corralled people into isolated parlour huddles for entertainment, groups like this were popular. He took daughter Gloria with him and at an early age she saw variety acts, singers and comedians amusing audiences. From before she was ten years old, she was on that stage singing – and she could sing well. During her school days she could be out four or five nights a week and not be back with her father until 2 a.m. No doubt about it, she had caught the showbiz bug.

When Gloria first presented herself some years later as a journalist broadcaster, there were those who wondered if this slip of a girl had sufficient background knowledge of what real life in troublesome areas was about. They probably didn't know that the Troubles of 1968–9 were not the first of which Gloria had some first-hand experience. Again from her own book, describing life on the variety concert road in the fifties: 'Mum was very perturbed at those journeys late at night in and around the border areas of Counties Armagh, Fermanagh and Tyrone. It was the time of the B-Specials in the fifties – an auxiliary group who assisted the Royal Ulster Constabulary, the Northern Ireland police force, to keep law and order in the border roads between north and south. When they waved their red-light torches, cars had to stop or they would open fire. I was always scared that our driver wouldn't see the light and we would be shot at.' Her father was teaching her perhaps more than he knew in those days.

But despatching Gloria to a typing class, where she spent part of the time with a bag over her head learning to touch type, gave her the means to skip through the doors of the new Ulster Television. She took an office job and then headed off to Canada to see a bit of the world. Her shorthand and typing skills landed her bread-and-butter jobs, but her singing and her Irish repertoire steered her towards exciting engagements on Canadian radio, leading to live concerts on the new television stations. So when she returned at the age of nineteen for a holiday in Portadown, she had more experience of performance on electronic media than many in the province. This was just as Ulster Television was advertising jobs, among them a job for a production assistant, or a PA, as they were often known in the business.

Gloria applied and was asked for interview, as she expected. By this time the local newspaper had printed a spread about her. At Ulster Television, however, she may have overplayed her young hand. She breezed in, oozing confidence as always, wearing a fur-lined hooded coat over a black dress she herself termed spectacular, brought back from Canada. To her disappointment, she did not get the PA job. Instead she was offered an office job in sales in Basil Lapworth's department. It was not what she wanted, but she thought she would take it for the meantime, while giving serious consideration to sailing back to Canada. It wasn't just radio and television that beckoned her back across the Atlantic. There was a man waiting for her there.

Soon after she arrived, Brum Henderson needed a secretary and she was deputed to serve. Brum never used a short word where a multisyllabic Latin derivative, preferably a harmonious cluster, could serve instead. As Gloria sat in his office, fearful of the presence, his first word was 'Felicitations!' What followed was elongated and similarly florid. Gloria wrote later: 'As his dictation progressed, it became clear that here was the most verbose man in the world.' When typing it up, she cut the wordage down to a third and he didn't seem to notice. I remember at the time there was a tale circulating in the aftermath of the Soviet leader Khrushchev's visit to Belgrade, then capital of Yugoslavia. Relations between the countries had been cool and everyone was being ultra-polite. Khrushchev told a long, involved joke without pausing for translation. The hapless interpreter uttered a couple of short sentences in Serbo-Croat, whereupon the Yugoslav hosts broke into loud laughter. Afterwards Khrushchev quietly asked the interpreter how his intricate, multi-layered tale could have been so succinctly relayed. The brave interpreter told him that he had said in Serbo-Croat, 'The First Secretary has just told a joke. You will all please laugh.' That interpreter and Gloria were cast from the same material.

Gloria and Brum seemed to click and she was able to tell him afterwards that she was the best sub-editor he ever had. He in turn gave her advice, such as: 'Never marry for money, but do your courting where there's a bit of it around.'

By this time, 'Roundabout' was getting into its stride and Gordon Duffield was making use of his filmic background to produce a programme called 'Preview', which did exactly what it said on the tin. This was before the outbreak of the Troubles and famous names were now turning up at the studio, top-flight entertainers such as Joe Loss and his orchestra, Emile Ford and the Checkmates, Acker Bilk and his band, along with actors of the stature of Richard Todd, Richard Harris and, yes, Beatrice Lillie. Film distributors were very keen to have television

Brum Henderson, chairman of the Royal Television Society (RTS) from 1982 to 1984, bestows the Royal Television Society's Gold Medal on Howard Steele in 1983. Howard Steele had been one of the consulting engineers for the new UTV in 1959. In the background, Sir Huw Weldon, President of the RTS, mooted in early days as a managing director of UTV.

promote their product and happily supplied both trailers and their stars under contract for Ulster Television. Sometimes they would head up afterwards to the Ram's Head on the Ormeau Road, but more often they would end up in the boardroom with its well-stocked drinks cabinet. Gloria noticed this and offered her services as a hostess free of charge in the evenings. She recalled, 'I soon made myself indispensable in the boardroom, chatting up the luminaries, making sure I always had my photo snapped with them by the studio photographer. Every weekend when I went home I'd produce the shots and tell my parents, "Guess who I met this week?"'

Gloria was not just mixing with the big names, she was mixing with UTV management and with programme producers and programme directors. Inevitably and persuasively, she got herself noticed. Perhaps equally inevitably, she was asked six weeks after joining whether she was still interested in a production assistant job, like the one she had originally applied for. Of course she was. Within a short time, a letter of farewell went to a sad young man in Canada, a man she would never see again. Gloria had got her foot in the desired door.

The PA job in television was and remains pivotal. It involved working closely with the producer, director and production team by attending and coordinating planning meetings; attending and timing rehearsals; overseeing timings during a shoot or show, cueing pre-recorded material; organising the production and distribution of scripts as well as, where necessary, typing up camera scripts and shot cards; producing timing schedules; liaising with the camera and sound crew during studio recordings; organising the captions (often called 'supers', normally identity captions shot on a black background and superimposed on an interviewee or on images of a place); checking copyright and permission issues and ensuring royalties were paid for images, music or footage; dealing with artists' payments and expenses; ensuring continuity where it mattered; sometimes dealing with production enquiries from the public; conducting research and completing all necessary paperwork in relation to the above tasks. In the early days there would not have been much work for a PA on an outside location, but if it happened, he or she was responsible for keeping accurate shot lists and logs for post-production. It was a bewildering mix of the menial, vital and complex. This was what Gloria took on.

'Roundabout' was critical to the success of Ulster Television. Brum had promised the regulator that it would be a successful and worthwhile programme. But he went further. He said that this single offering could also be in part a testing ground for programme ideas that could be developed into additional local programmes, as soon as finances allowed. It was not just a matter of keeping the ITA off their backs. Brum assumed the managing directorship at the beginning of 1960 at the ripe old age of thirty, which was only ten years older than Gloria. Now he had also to manage public expectations because the company's promises about programmes were in the public domain. A measure of those public expectations lay in what the *Belfast Telegraph* wrote just before the opening: 'The initials UTV . . . will suddenly assume an important new significance . . . as the symbol of an Ulster company's own assessment of Ulster prestige, intelligence and culture'. This symbol would be represented in the first period by one local programme, 'Roundabout'. The paper added that it expected an increase in local airtime before Christmas. WH Wilson, who was the ITA regional officer based in Belfast as UTV began, did add a note of caution to his masters in London when he wrote: 'I do not think we can expect a lot in the formative months. How many formative months there are going to be, I would not like to say!' The ITA continued to consider Ulster Television as something of an experiment, not altogether convinced it could survive commercially. The Authority would tread carefully. Brum knew this, but he also knew that the pressure was on the company from more than just the ITA.

Gloria Hunniford with a karate practitioner for her groundbreaking programme, 'Good Evening Ulster', which began in 1979. It lasted a full hour from six in the evening and was a mix of hard news and softer items.

Early in Ulster Television's history, the up-and-coming broadcaster David Frost visited Northern Ireland. The occasion was deemed sufficiently significant for the UTV managing director himself to interview the great man.

Very quickly, therefore, the company got more programming on air. Relatively speaking, studio programmes, as distinct from filmed programmes, were cheap, so into the afternoons came 'A Matter of Taste', an hour-long programme aimed at the woman in the home. It ended a mere 30 minutes before 'Roundabout' began, and since there was only one small studio, it had to be a quick turnaround. Not least for Gloria, because there was only one PA on duty for any period of the day. This was shoestring television, as Gloria describes: 'At half past five I'd gather up all my captions, theme music, timing notes and contracts, and race upstairs to my office, dumping it all and lifting the next bundle for the news programme at 6 p.m. You had to be on top of it. I was calling the shots, back timing the programme, which meant I had to know all the camera line-ups and crossovers. Of course, it was all splendid training for the future. To this day, the one thing I can do as a broadcaster is read a clock.' Unlike the celebrated Jack de Manio, who around the same time in London became the presenter of the breakfast-time 'Today' programme. Jack became notorious for wrong time-checks to an audience racing against the clock to get to work. When he eventually left the BBC, they did not give him the traditional watch: they gave him the studio clock.

Gloria also had to work on advertising magazines, or 'admags', as they were known, a feature unique to British television and from which Ulster Television was not immune. They only lasted until 1963 and from today's perspective, it is a wonder they lasted that long. They were like mini-soaps, about a quarter of an hour long, and scripted by the ITV company making them, with product names dropped into the spoken lines and woven into contrived stories, as if by accident. 'Oh look, Gerald. You have almost spilt the healthy, calcium-filled Milk Marketing Board milk with the delicious Kellogg's Corn Flakes all over my wonderfully-cut Parsons and Parsons Donegal tweed jacket. Get me the Dettol, which will have this clean and sweet-smelling in a minute. No no, Gerald. That's the remarkably effective Head and Shoulders shampoo, darling. Absolutely wonderful for my hair but not for this . . .' That is not a real sample and probably a little over the top, but it gives the idea. The references in reality needed to be more drawn out, because advertisers were paying for their product in shot – usually for between 15 and 20 seconds – and more words were needed about each product. Gloria wondered how the UTV admag actors managed to keep straight faces.

Execrable though these admags were, they nevertheless held a fascination for the viewer. The fact that they were just about the only local drama on screen may have had something to do with it. Companies like UTV were happy with them because they did not count towards the advertising minutes-per-hour allowed by the ITA. They were therefore extra revenue. And, of course, they were live – no electronic recording in the early sixties. Because they were live and because all the products had to be within easy reach, there was not much scope with the format. In turn, this required the admags to be themed. Fanny and John Craddock, the original television cooks, featured in cookery-themed admags alongside Philip Harben and Marguerite Patton.

Each admag would encompass a number of products, so the script had to be an agreed effort between all participating advertisers, something of a task when each believed his product ought to dominate. And all of them seemed to want nothing but close-ups. Jo Gable, in her book, *The Tuppenny Punch and Judy Show*, related a hilarious unforeseen consequence of this mania for close-ups: 'Remembering his admag days one director recalled the occasion when he had to film a chunk of Spam dressed with mayonnaise. The Spam representative demanded closer and closer shots of the Spam until the director felt he was right into the pores of this lump of meat. At that moment, a bluebottle landed on the mayonnaise and, because of the magnification, appeared on the television screens like some grotesque, carbuncled monster.' It was live and there was nothing the Spam man could do about it.

The Pilkington Committee on Broadcasting brought down the admag. It reported in 1962 that the admags were blurring the distinction between advertisements and programmes, even though they were clearly labelled as advertising. Pilkington also objected to the fact that the admags allowed in effect more advertising than was permitted by the law and that the programmes were so close to sponsored programmes that the distinction was barely discernible. The tide turned against them and by 1963, they were gone. But not completely, in the minds of some. The successor to admags might be product placement or product integration, which is when a product is used in a television or film shot, perhaps in a drama, because someone has paid for it to be there. Currently this is not allowed on British television. But Sir Michael Grade, chairman of ITV Plc, told a

'The Humour is on Me Now', an early programme on culture introduced by Denis Ireland and James Boyce. *From left*: Denis Ireland (writer), Kitty Gibson (actress), James Boyce (broadcaster) and Roy Johnston (folk singer).

House of Lords Committee on Broadcasting in 2009 that product placement is 'all over screens in the US and I don't see any civil unrest or people marching in the streets over Bond films being shown or 'Desperate Housewives'. It's just nonsense – we've got to get real.'

However, in the early sixties, Ulster Television found it could get along without the admags. By the end of 1961 advertising sales had passed the 1 million mark, dispelling once and for all the pessimism at the start-up of some of the directors. By the end of 1962, profits were over a quarter of a million pounds. The directors felt so buoyant that they felt they had to report that their good sales had been achieved without any obvious effect on the prosperity of other advertising media in Northern Ireland. Already the company had bought the property adjacent to Havelock House with a view to expansion. UTV had achieved a share of more than two thirds of the total viewing audience since beginning transmissions. The

Scene from a documentary about the Belfast *News Letter*, August 1987. Captain O.W.J. Henderson, often referred to as Captain Bill, seen leafing through files, is the brother of Brum Henderson.

growth in the number of television sets in the first year was startling, with a dramatic increase of over 50 per cent. UTV claimed with justification 'that Independent Television has made a successful debut with the Ulster public. The amount of locally originated programmes has been doubled within a short period, and these programmes have proved more popular with our public than has been the case elsewhere.'

Added to that was a feather in the cap. 'Roundabout' was being regarded as a resounding success beyond the shores of Northern Ireland. In the January after Ulster Television's launch, the Dublin Senate debated the Bill that would introduce a television service for the Republic. One speaker advocated co-operation with neighbouring broadcasting authorities, because he thought the programmes shown in Northern Ireland were 'extraordinarily effective in their Irish local flavour'. As early as September of UTV's first year, the ITA director general was referring to 'Roundabout' as a remarkable programme whose unique success led to its being copied in other ITV regions, mentioning Scotland, Wales and the northeast of England. Out of necessity, Ulster Television had invented the regional current affairs magazine! It was a better beginning than anyone on either the Ulster Television board or the Independent Television Authority had dared hope for.

About this time Gloria met Don Keating, who had joined UTV as a cameraman and risen to become a television director. They got married in the spring of 1961 and, in accordance with the custom of the day, Gloria had to leave Ulster Television. Husband and wife were not allowed to work in the same department. She began a family and resumed her singing career. But Gloria wasn't away for long. She returned, only this time in front of camera as a singer on 'Teatime with Tommy'.

UTV took 'Tommy', Tommy James, on the road. Jim Creagh, who ended his career as assistant managing director and who for many years was in charge of the station's public image, was once on one of these tours, which had everything to do with station promotion. He remembers one evening in Carrickmore, where Tommy was billed to conduct a talent show at eight in the evening in the local hall. By eight not a soul had appeared, much to the consternation of the whole production crew. Jim remembers standing in the wings, peeping out at the rows of empty seats, by his side the 'clapometer', which he 'operated' to signify the support of each contestant. The local priest said not to worry. People would come. At 8.15 p.m. there was no one. 'Don't worry', was the message from the priest. No one at 8.30 p.m. or 8.45 p.m. In the background, the priest was sanguine, even cheery. 'Don't worry,' he repeated. He said the same at 9.00 p.m. and at 9.15 p.m., by which time Tommy, Jim and the UTV crew thought that the priest was an amiable but incorrigible self-deluded romantic, and that they should be packing up. Not a solitary person was in evidence and the priest was still infuriatingly optimistic. But he was right. At 9.30 p.m. the hall was packed, ready for the fun. 'It's a very rural community,' the priest explained. 'Folk here have to finish work on the farms and then get their best Sunday clothes on. It takes a little time. Eight o'clock is a bit early for them.' It all ended at about two in the morning. Jim left amazed at many things that night, not least the number of pubs in Carrickmore.

This easy, simple music programme with the gentle Tommy James behind the piano became a favourite of the audiences. The format was for people to write in to request their chosen song, and Gloria and other singers would dutifully render it to Tommy's piano accompaniment. She had other work too. In 1964 something of a nightclub or cabaret scene was beginning in Belfast, with the rise of venues like the Abercorn and Talk of the Town, where a young entertainer called Roy Walker was beginning his career.

Then the Troubles began in or around 1969, and travelling to and from venues at night became a problem. Keeping the venues open at all became a problem, in fact. The result was yet another change of gear through the auspices of a highly regarded radio current affairs producer in BBC Belfast called Dan Gilbert. For Gloria, the cabaret business was collapsing and Dan spied a talent. She became a radio reporter for his programme and in 1972 found herself back at the Abercorn bar in the middle of Belfast. A bomb exploded on a Saturday afternoon, killing two young women and injuring over 100 innocent people. It was one of the most notorious explosions of the Troubles. On another occasion, Gloria reported from the Grand Central Hotel, where Sir Laurence Olivier had stayed when opening UTV. Now it was an Army base.

A couple of years later our paths crossed again, as I took up the position as head of radio at BBC Belfast. I had just come from Downtown Radio, the province's first commercial radio station, where I had been the inaugural programme controller. Downtown Radio had severely diminished BBC Radio Ulster's audience, which, paradoxically enough, became a reason why I was employed by the BBC. The only programme on BBC radio which had given me a run for my money was 'Taste of Hunni', Gloria's one-hour show. The first thing I did on entering my new office was double her airtime, something that should have happened long before I appeared. She was a natural with people, both low and high. She looked great and carried herself like a star. Furthermore, she knew about music. That kind of combination only comes along once in a while.

Occasionally Gloria dropped a clanger. Her producer was Ian Kennedy, now with Skillset Northern Ireland. At one time, she had torn ligaments in her leg and

Programme director Maureen White with presenter Hugh Owens in the *News Letter* archives while making the 1987 documentary about the newspaper. The paper began publishing in 1737.

was walking with the aid of a crutch, which she had by her side in the studio. She was live on air and Ian was kneeling on the floor, sorting out music discs, which her crutch lay over. Suddenly he heard Gloria saying into the mike, 'You should see my producer grovelling under my crotch looking for the next record.' The studio engineer dissolved into incoherent laughter and Ian simply went grey. She tried to explain and correct to 'crutch', but it only seemed to make things worse. We had only one complaint from a lady who thought the programme was tending to depravity. But no. 'Taste of Hunni' went from strength to strength until one day, like all good things, it came to an end.

I remember sensing it when the programme team, along with myself, ended up at a delightful inn at Fahan, just over the border in Donegal from Derry/Londonderry, or 'Stroke City', as broadcaster Gerry Anderson wisely dubbed the place. It was just after a successful outside broadcast and the weather was warm and beautiful. The group of us were on the lawn overlooking the sea and all should have been wonderful. But I felt the chill. Gloria was more reserved than usual. I guessed what must be happening in the background and resigned myself to the fact that we were not going to be able to hold on to this talent for ever. Indeed, neither was Northern Ireland.

The seventies in Northern Ireland were a bleak, dark decade, something Gloria had seen firsthand for herself. She had even been in a studio in Derry when the building was bombed. 1979 began badly, with an IRA bomb blitz across several towns on New Year's Day. The rest of the year was a litany of murder and destruction and the consequences thereof. The Bennett Report said there had been ill-treatment of suspects in Castlereagh police station; eleven members of the Shankill Butchers gang were convicted of 112 offences including nineteen murders; eighteen soldiers were killed in a landmine explosion near Warrenpoint, and Lord Mountbatten, on holiday at Mullaghmore in Co. Sligo, was assassinated by the IRA. There was talk of political initiatives but there was also a widespread feeling that it was all posturing and hot air. There was no optimism. If ever a place needed a psychological pick-me-up, it was surely Northern Ireland. Ulster Television provided one in the shape of 'Good Evening Ulster'.

'Good Evening Ulster', presented by Gloria Hunniford, was a landmark programme for Ulster Television. It lasted a full hour and was a mix of hard news, of which there was plenty, and softer items, for which the production team had to delve and manufacture. It was exactly the blend that a battered audience required. Viewers had to have the news, of course, but UTV management realised that the unrelieved diet of reporting on the violence and political sparring was becoming overwhelming. There was some opposition to having someone like Gloria front what still needed to be in large part a news programme, but her radio reporting experience now stood her in good stead.

The programme wiped the floor with any opposition and UTV was delighted. So, when Gloria said she would like to do the programme from New York on St Patrick's Day in 1980, management said yes. As broadcaster Gerry Kelly, who was working on the programme and who went to New York with her, said, 'If she had wanted to do a programme from the moon, they might have said yes.' Ian Sanderson, the programme editor, had gone ahead to plan interviews, but when

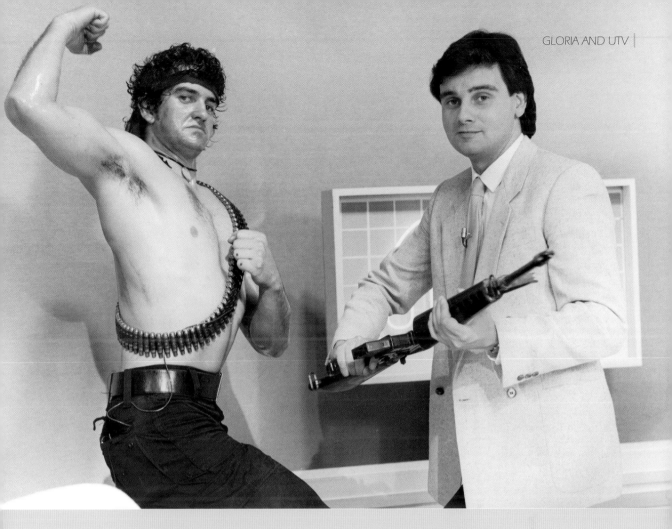

Eamonn Holmes is yet another national broadcasting figure whose television career was launched at Havelock House, when he became a presenter on 'Good Evening Ulster'. Here he is interviewing comedian Sammy Mackie about his spoof Rambo record in 1983.

Gloria arrived, she was a bit disappointed with the line-up. Within minutes, from information in her contact book, she had secured an interview with Mia Farrow. That phone call encapsulated why Gloria was where she was and why UTV prized her above all others. As Brum Henderson said, 'Television attracts many dilettantes but we in Ulster Television have been lucky enough to attract many real pros. She is one of them.'

'Good Evening Ulster' lasted less than three years. Radio Ulster could not retain Gloria for long and neither could Ulster Television. Gloria moved on to fame as a national broadcaster.

Chapter 8

Hello new broom, goodbye old Brum

1983 happens to be almost halfway to Ulster Television's golden jubilee, but it was also a turning point in the history of the company. It was the year that Brum Henderson, long regarded as the father of the station, moved positions from managing director and deputy chairman to chairman. A new man, Desmond Smyth, moved into Brum's old seat behind the managing director's desk. It was also the year when a new young person came into the management of the company. His name was John McCann.

Brum Henderson wrote two books about television, this being the first.

John McCann qualified as an accountant with Ernst & Young and then joined the rescue division of IDB, forerunner to Invest Northern Ireland. 'I spent a couple of fascinating years there,' he says. ' If you want to know what makes a company tick, there is no better way than to examine what is happening when a company is going down the tubes.' Desmond Smyth had been the financial controller and when he was promoted, John McCann took over his job. It did not take long for McCann to make his mark. He was only six months in the job when the man in charge of industrial relations left. UTV's industrial relations were described at the time both inside and outside the company as a nightmare. Nobody on the UTV management team wanted the poisoned chalice, so McCann took it for what he thought was a temporary term: 'I actually had the notion that if reasonable men sat around a table, they could reach reasonable conclusions. I was like a lamb to the slaughter. For the first six months the unions ran rings round me. After that, I got the hang of it and decided that we could not continue the way we were going.'

The television industry was notorious for 'Spanish practices' which had grown up over the years. When the industry moved over to colour back in the seventies, the unions had demanded a pay rise, including a rise for sound recordists. 'Colour sound', it was termed without humour by the unions. A good example of how the system was being abused was at closedown each night. The station was scheduled to go off the air at a specific time, but if closedown was delayed by 3 minutes, then the technical staff on duty received double time for the shift they had just worked. Needless to say, night after night reasons were found to delay closedown sufficiently to claim double time. It was so easy to play out a programme trail tape or two. There were transmission controllers on enormous take-home pay. The more McCann looked at the situation, the more he believed it could not go on:

> My view was that we had to resolve these issues or we did not have a future, meaning the company or the industry. I knew that at some stage there would have to be a strike, a test of wills. Television airtime is a more perishable commodity than fruit. When the airtime is gone, it is gone and it cannot be recreated, so if the workforce takes you off the air, that airtime is gone forever. Your costs were pretty fixed and therefore not like making cars. If the car industry suffered a strike, management could cut costs by cancelling supplies, such as sheet metal, until production resumed. A silent factory, though not without cost, is not consuming at the same rate as when in full production. With television, the costs remain static whether or not you are selling airtime.

The unions knew that ITV management had become scared of ever being off the air, so there was little need to bother with negotiation. They just stated what they wanted.

In these years, the early and mid-eighties, ITV was in a position of monopoly. There was Channel 4, but ITV sold its airtime, so it was no commercial competition. In that situation, it was relatively easy to make money in ITV. However, it was easier for those who had come in from the outside, like McCann, to see that the bountiful days were bound to end. Those who had grown up with the system found that less easy to perceive, so McCann had only lukewarm support from some management colleagues in locking horns with the unions.

Brum Henderson had never confronted the unions. 'The union guys I dealt with talked about going up the back stairs if they did not get what they wanted from the line managers,' McCann explains. 'Back stairs was code for going to Brum. But Brum was not alone in that. Many of the ITV managers would have been alongside him.'

Desmond Smyth, managing director. UTV has had only four managing directors: Bill MacQuitty, Brum Henderson, Desmond, and the present managing director, John McCann.

Under McCann's influence, UTV was now taking the lead throughout the ITV network in making a stand, so that by 1986 this small company was having more serious disputes than the rest of the network combined. Desmond Smyth was being pressurised by the ITV director of industrial relations, John Calvert, to calm things down. Fresh in John's memory, and that of all ITV management, was the memory of an extended strike which put the whole of ITV off the air in 1979 from August to October, with programmes being replaced by a simple white-on-blue caption apologising for the loss of service. Locally important events UTV missed because it was off air were the visit to Ireland by the Pope and the terrible day when Lord Mountbatten and his party were blown up in a Sligo bay and eighteen soldiers died in a mine explosion outside Warrenpoint.

However, in the mid-eighties, the political background was one of confrontation with the unions. Margaret Thatcher was Prime Minister, the Iron Lady who had won the Falkland's war and then taken on the powerful National Union of Miners and won. The times were propitious for John McCann's strategy.

By now, McCann had the bit between his teeth and was preparing for outright war with the unions. He recruited a new personnel manager for UTV, John Hutchinson, and then he did something interesting: 'I put myself on a one-week course in the south of England for new people to the industry, such as production assistants. [I] remember, on the first morning, the self-introductions round the class. One was a PA, the other was a floor manager, another a technician and then it came to me. I said, "Ulster Television's financial controller", and that I wanted to familiarise myself a little with the production side of the company.' The others stared at him because it was a rigid rule throughout that management touched nothing technical. Next, McCann quietly put John Hutchinson through the same course, then a few other non-technical managers. The aim was to garner sufficient expertise to keep the station on air in the circumstances of a walk-out. Once that happened, the network signal would be cut by the unions. There were be nothing to fall back upon. No network, no 'Coronation Street', no ITN news, no drama, no nothing!

When that happened, UTV would need something to show. 'I decided to buy material from elsewhere and, for example, I secretly bought the series "V". I stored the cans in garages or under beds to be used in the event of a strike and our losing the network signal.' Any of the 1986 confrontations could have taken the station off the air but it turned out to be a peculiarly local difficulty which provided the catalyst.

The powerful union of the time was the ACTT, and its UTV shop steward also had a pub in Killyleagh. The company discovered that while claiming to be ill, he was working in his pub. However, this man was the chairman of the national negotiating committee, a most powerful figure in the union who may have believed he was bulletproof. At a meeting attended by national union officers shortly before Easter 1987, UTV management declared bluntly that they were firing the man in question. There was palpable shock. This kind of treatment was not meted out to union officers, not even when they were pulling pints instead of being at work. The union people stormed out of the meeting and shortly after, the technical staff walked out of the station. Battle was joined. What happened next has become folk history within the company.

For three days the station was dark, as the management explored the relatively unknown technical areas and began to familiarise themselves with the machines. UTV did not even attempt to take network programmes from across the water and broadcast them. It would have been a waste of time. Furthermore, the rest of ITV did not want embroiled in this UTV dispute. 'The strikers probably thought we would not be able to work the apparatus,' says McCann. 'I can recall standing in front of one of those big telecine machines. We had its glass door open trying to figure out what path the film took among the sprocket wheels. If we could not get it to work, our plans to beat the strike would fall apart. Then someone said, "Try this," and simply closed the glass door. Suddenly it worked. For safety reasons, the machine would not go unless the door was closed.'

🔲 Havelock House as it looks today with some of the modern extensions. In the background are the remains of the old gasworks, which caused engineers technical problems.

After three days the management were ready and began a schedule from six in the evening until ten. It mostly went well, but not always. During the film *Support Your Local Sheriff!*, the bangs came after the cowboy had put the gun back in the holster. It was a comedy western, but not supposed to be *that* funny. Some of the training happened on air. John McCann was operating the video tape machine when cued by Andy Crockart, who was directing. The cue came but Andy accidentally selected the wrong switch. From the monitor, John saw what had happened and stopped the video to rewind it. But as soon as he did so, Andy had no means of recovering, because now the video tape pictures were not there to be found. The professionals would have kept the tape running to allow the director to find it. The damage is reduced that way. But with each mishap, more was being learnt.

One member of management put it this way: 'The biggest mistake the union made was having that strike. Once the management of UTV got into the sacrosanct technical area, they discovered how easy it was to spool up, to route a signal and to press "go" when required. Very quickly managers were asking about the degree of difficulty and complication that required the huge rates of pay after midnight. Before the strike we were not allowed near a machine.'

They did run some advertising. Paul Hutchinson, Ireland advertising director, describes what was done: 'We had some advertisers who had declared an interest in being on air at this period. We had their copy in the building. We told them we would charge them what they had previously agreed, but not for extra showings. If they had paid for twenty transmissions and got eighty, so be it. They did not complain.'

Brum Henderson, by now chairman, made enemies among his own hard-pressed management during the strike. Many mornings there would be long memos to Desmond Smyth, criticising the previous night's output, saying there was a flaw here, a flaw there. Desmond showed the complaints to John McCann and they both agreed not to show them to the rest of the management because of the effect upon their morale. Managers and sales staff were working a full day, then working with unfamiliar equipment to maintain a service during the evening, getting back to their homes between ten and eleven at night, every night. They were becoming very tired. If the strikers had known just how tired they were, they might have held out.

But the strikers blinked first, and at the end of a two-week period the men said they would come back to work, and restoring the pub man was not a pre-condition. McCann told the strikers that if they embarked upon a war of attrition, UTV would win. The alternative was to work together but he wanted a local deal, not one brokered in London. 'Then people came to their senses and people settled down. The company began to prosper, notwithstanding the competition. That was the transformation we wanted,' McCann remembers. A walk-out threat from the unions had lost much of its punch.

The battle and its outcome at UTV may have affected strategy at TV-am, where later in the year a six-month battle with the unions began. Technically it was a lockout rather than a strike, but either way the station ran the same way UTV did during their strike. Margaret Thatcher had referred to TV as being the last bastion of restrictive practices. She used to handbag the ITV managing directors, including Desmond Smyth. She saw what was happening when television crews came to interview her: lots of people who had barely definable jobs. She realised that this was a side effect of monopolies, and that ITV could continue charging the advertisers for the restrictive practices.

However, the two-week strike was the making of John McCann. Had he lost, he would have been out the door. But having won, he was now well regarded by colleagues and board members. The law of unintentional consequences now came into play. A side effect was that John had fashioned for himself the beginnings of a power base for the next crucial internal struggle, which was to see Brum Henderson leave the business.

It is tempting to view the demise of Brum Henderson in terms of the young Turk elbowing out the old guy. However, it was not as simple as that. There were others drawing a bead on Brum some years before John McCann joined UTV.

Back in 1980, Brum Henderson's position was a talking point within the regulator, the IBA. Having said that, the IBA collectively had a mixed view of the ITV managing directors and chairs, many of whom the regulator thought made rods for their own backs. The classic case of this was by Roy Thomson of Scottish Television, who famously and publicly said in the early days that running a television company was like having a licence to print money. If ever there was an invitation to government to windfall tax an industry, this was it. And sure enough, that is what government did some years later. Alan Bremner, later to be programme controller of Ulster Television, joined the IBA just before the 1980 contract round, when companies had to re-apply for their licences, and he was party to inner thinking about Ulster Television and Brum Henderson in particular.

'Much of the discussion was on whether Brum was a force for good or a dead hand,' says Bremner. 'I remember being quite taken aback by the idea that he was a dead hand. The general perception of UTV by the IBA at that time was that you had this fearsome autocracy, fiercely money driven, which was not spending much on programmes. There was concern that UTV was perceived in Northern Ireland as being too Orange, even though the programmes were not Orange.'

In the run-up period to the awarding of the licences, there was within the IBA a period of what was known as 'purdah', when contact with the existing companies was technically restricted, so as to avoid giving the impression that challengers for the contract were disadvantaged. It was one of those ideas germinating from bureaucratic introspection that had more meaning in the proposition than in the execution, a piece of administrative contortion prompted by an unreasoned fear that the world outside was prepared to believe that officers of a regulator might be acting unfairly in some way because they were seen smiling unnecessarily at a company executive. In the real world, IBA officers had to maintain normal contact, as required by the Broadcasting Act. Ofcom, the successor regulatory body, maintains the idea of purdah rules to this day.

The purdah regime led to odd incidents, where off-the-cuff remarks could be invested with great meaning. For example, the IBA decided in 1980 to visit Belfast and there was great debate as to whether to accept an invitation to lunch at UTV because that would 'compromise the objectivity of the licence process'. But in the end they did accept. Brum made a generous if anxious speech, but criticised in a veiled way the finality of the process. At one stage he remarked that it was a most difficult job, being a surgeon. From her seated position, Lady Plowden, the distinguished educationalist who was chair of the IBA, muttered audibly, 'And if necessary, Brum, I will amputate a limb.'

'That raised the anxiety factor considerably,' says Bremner, who was present, 'because of what she had said and how she had said it. I can remember the chill that went round the table. Brum went through a week afterwards, wondering if he had completely cocked it up and jeopardised his position.' The real meaning of the remark was probably to be found in purdah-offset. It was almost as if receiving UTV hospitality was acceptable, as long as a senior IBA person said something nasty to a senior UTV person.

As the day for interviewing the applicant companies by the IBA approached, Colin Shaw and David Glencross, the two most senior people in the programming department of the IBA, intervened with a very powerful note implying that they were fed up with this notion of Brum being perceived as a dead hand. They believed this man had an energy which, if properly channelled, could be used for the good of UTV.

UTV management had no idea until long afterwards of the extraordinary events on the day they went to be interviewed in London. Alan Bremner learnt of it from within the IBA. The UTV interview at the IBA in London happened in the morning. However, in the afternoon Frank Brady, the UTV chief engineer, requested a private meeting in the IBA with Sir Brian Young, director general, and Lady Plowden. To their astonishment, he begged them not to give the licence to UTV, saying that Brum was a tyrant not to be trusted with it. This was the same Frank Brady on whose behalf Brum Henderson had interceded all those years ago, in order to procure him a work permit and thereby his UTV job. We will never know what motivated Frank Brady. Both he and Brum are dead.

The two people at the highest level of the IBA were now in a very awkward position because they had agreed to a meeting with a disaffected figure within the management of an applicant group. They now had evidence that the management of UTV was divided. But what status could they confer upon the informal, indeed secret, meeting with Frank Brady? Shaw and Glencross said it had to be discounted. In the end, after consultation with the IBA member for Northern Ireland, Billy Blease, Lord Blease of Cromac, the IBA agreed within its own debating arenas that no action could be taken against UTV. However, the incident had happened and had damaged Brum, as was undoubtedly intended.

It was made clear to UTV that in returning the license to the company, there was an expectation that Brum Henderson was to be eased out of the position of managing director. This was put in writing to UTV.

All this happened before 1983, which is when John McCann came into the company, recruited by Desmond Smyth, whom Brum had appointed to the managing directorship. By then Brum was company chairman, which was seen as adherence to the IBA wish. Brum and John McCann never saw eye to eye on anything. 'He and I clashed very early on,' John recalls. 'He called me "Limb of Satan" in a charming way, saying that I had nine lives like a cat, while reminding me I had just used up another. But I used up more than nine.'

The working methods of the two men differed substantially. Brum liked written reports which he could study. John McCann kept written communication to a minimum, preferring to walk down the corridor and talk or use the phone. So when he attended one of the industry's big shows in the United States, NAB, John returned, told people what he had seen of interest and settled down once more behind his desk. Brum then asked Desmond for a written report on NAB and

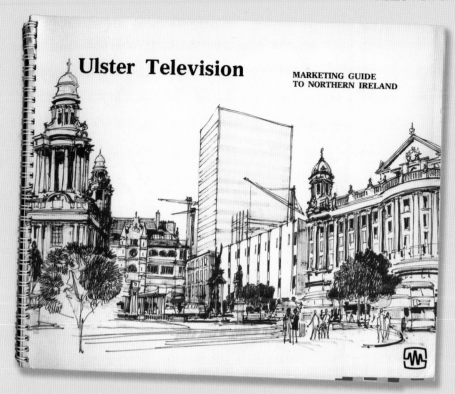

The UTV marketing guide, 1975. It stated that the effect of civil unrest had been marginal on the economy. The tone was upbeat, with an introduction that concluded: 'There is great potential for economic growth in Northern Ireland when inflation is reduced and "the Troubles" are over and the next upswing of the UK economy gets under way.'

Desmond asked McCann – who said he had better uses for his time. Desmond asked McCann for the sake of peace to do a report, but no report appeared. Brum did not ask McCann directly for the report.

A dinner was subsequently arranged for UTV management at Brum's home in Ballynahinch. There were two tables because of the numbers, one hosted by Brum and the other by Mrs Henderson. John McCann had a pleasant evening at the table hosted by Mrs Henderson; Mrs McCann was at Brum's table.

When the McCanns got into their car to go home, John's wife, Máiréad, said, 'You wouldn't believe what Brum said to me. Were you supposed to do some sort of report? Because Brum said to me, "Your husband is a terrible man. I have been trying to get him to give me a report and he won't do it."'

Brum never did receive that report. And trying to get it through a wife did not improve relations between the two men. It was interesting that at no time did Brum ask John McCann directly for the report. Brum was still spooked by the strike and he was certainly anxious about the growing control of the executives.

Brian Waddell, controller of local programmes since 1976, had been promoted to the board three years later. Brian had come through the ranks and knew programme-making thoroughly. In the fifties he had started work as a journalist in the *Newtownards Chronicle* after taking an arts degree at Queen's University. He moved to the *Northern Whig*, then a Belfast daily paper, where he became motoring editor. When Ulster Television came along, Brian suggested doing motoring stories for 'Roundabout' to producer John Shultz Conway. He then worked with Fred Corbett and Paddy Scott as a motoring freelance and got the next assistant editor job on the programme. They had limited film effort because at the time there was no film processing at UTV, so they made do with slides. But when film was needed, Sean McGaffin took the shots on his mute Bolex clockwork camera, which was an excellent piece of equipment and a mainstay of news and feature filming on all TV stations at the time. The camera never faltered, but Brian wondered how Sean survived: 'He never had a coat, just a wee jacket always soaking with bottles of stout.'

Brian moved into programme direction and into the field of entertainment, turning his hand to anything that UTV was doing, such as 'Teatime with Tommy': 'We would record five of Tommy's programmes over Saturday and Sunday. Tommy's trio were very popular indeed, but it was a stint we did not like. Not because of Tommy, who was charming and professional: it was simply such a chore turning these things out. The programmes were recorded on two-inch tape which you could not edit, so we had to record-as-live. If there was a hiccup or a fluff you either had to go back to the beginning or live with it.'

Over the years, Brian Waddell made a host of programmes both as producer and as director, including, in 1970, UTV's first full-length colour documentary, 'No Surrender', about, as you may have already guessed, the Orange Order. The whole network was bit by bit moving to colour and this programme was made while the station was still broadcasting in black and white. Unusually for UTV programmes, it was shown over most of the ITV network.

Three years later, Brian produced the 'The Gordon Burns Hour' on Saturday nights. Gordon Burns had already left UTV to further his career in England, but returned for a chat show that must have prepared some ground for the very long-running 'Kelly' programme at the end of the next decade. The Burns programme pioneered a live programme link between Belfast and Dublin. 'To drop a network programme on a Saturday night and put in your own show was a big step,' says Brian.

'We did very well in getting big names to come across. Our greatest experiment was joining up with Gay Byrne and 'The Late Late Show'. The two were on at roughly the same time. We came to a point in the middle when we would join the two by both going into a commercial break. It was enormously difficult. Our biggest problem was to get Gay to stick to what had been arranged. But if things were going well for him he would simply forget about the commercial, while UTV did enter one. It became quite edgy at times between Burns and Gay when we were messed about like that.'

In the end, while they found Gay generally a nice man to work with, they abandoned the link. It was too difficult.

Brian could also lay claim to bringing two important presenters to Ulster Television. One was David Dunseith, now with the BBC: 'I remember David coming from the Drugs Squad for interview in the studio. I was producing and I was impressed with the way he handled the studio so afterwards I asked if he had ever thought of a career in TV. He said he had a career in the police, but six months later he changed his mind and joined UTV. He had a very inquisitive mind and a sympathy with the people – and was photogenic. We worked together for a long time.'

The other name was Gloria Hunniford. 'Brum claims Gloria was his idea, but I had been talking to Gloria for a long time because her programme on Radio Ulster was doing very well,' says Brian. 'At first she was not inclined to move. But finally she said she would have a go. There had been a lot of discussion inside Havelock House about this. We were launching a new hour-long teatime programme and there were those who said that it should be fronted by a journalist, given that we were in the middle of the Troubles.' Gloria went on to prove that there was little in the panoply of broadcasting formats that she could not handle. UTV won hands down with the new programme. 'Choosing a presenter is very much a seat-of-pants matter,' Brian admitted.

Brian and Brum worked closely together for a couple of decades, but it was not easy to be a programme controller under Brum. 'He wanted to be programme controller as well as managing director,' says Brian. 'As time went on he did give me my head and allowed me to do what I thought was right. With his blessing, of course. He was a hard task master, very difficult. Yet a very good friend. And he was great in company.'

Sir Harry Secombe at the Ulster American Folk
Park with one of its progenitors, Eric Montgomery,
one-time head of the Stormont information
service. The museum records eighteenth- and
nineteenth-century emigration from Ulster to
America.

Brian can give an insight into Brum's attitude towards the IBA. Commercial television in the United Kingdom was in a sense an odd business. It depended on one crucial contract, and therefore on one crucial relationship – that with the regulator, who handed out the programme contract. Without that piece of paper, a programme contract company, as the IBA termed them, just disappeared or transformed itself into another type of company. Thames Television, for example, became an independent supplier of network programmes when it lost the franchise, using the expertise it had built up over years.

Once a year the IBA carried out a review of each of the fifteen ITV companies. It was both a review and a preview of what was in store. These events pressurised Brum. He would bring Brian up to the boardroom, draft and redraft the submission, rehearse and rehearse and generally work himself up. Then, in late autumn, Brian and Brum would head for London and the meeting with the IBA programme people, including Colin Shaw and David Glencross. There was a ritual. The two UTV executives would enter the IBA offices, say their piece, answer questions and leave. They went immediately round the corner to the Hyde Park Hotel and had a great lunch in the grill. But it scarcely compensated Brum for the blood, sweat and perhaps even tears he had expended. Brum Henderson accorded the IBA much respect. 'If there was a communication from the IBA, Brum got excited and worried. Then the rest of us worried,' Brian says.

This goes some way towards explaining what in the end happened to Brum within the company. But only some way. A major part of what happened was the erosion of his own power base internally. For example, he lost Brian, who, though he clearly exasperated him occasionally, supported Brum.

In 1988 Brian was beginning to feel that he had lived through the halcyon days of UTV: 'Most important was that ITV and UTV were cash rich and that made a heck of a difference to programmers. Money was not a problem. The freedom that we had!' (It was during this period of plenty that UTV began its celebrated art collection.) But Brian sensed that the freedom would be ending. He was correct to do so.

For some time both McCann and Smyth had been unhappy with programme-makers walking into meetings and declaring that this or that programme had been made or was in the making. The two managers thought that there was no appetite for costcutting among programme-makers, and even less appetite for allowing others in the company to have an input into deciding what programmes should be made. Since programmes were the only product made by the company, aside from some advertisements, both managers felt that they needed more of a handle on that side of the business. Before Alan Bremner had left the IBA, he had quietly told John McCann that the IBA thought the programmes were bland and unexciting, which also fuelled their discontent.

Alan Bremner saw immediately on joining the company that a showdown was on the way about what programmes needed to be made and about how money was spent. Brian Waddell was by now fifty-five, was director of programmes and probably had no enthusiasm for the tussles that loomed on the horizon. However, his enthusiasm for programme-making was as strong as ever. He was eyeing the new role of independent producer or programme-maker, which was just forming, and television organisations would be buying programmes from them. Five years down the line, when he would be leaving UTV anyway for retirement, a raft of independent producers would already have a foothold. Time to get out and start my own business, thought Brian. He left, and within nine months his company was making 20 hours for the UTV evening magazines. Today Waddell Media is a large independent production company with an office in New York.

Brum had had two senior allies among the executives: Brian Waddell and Jim Creagh, head of publicity and assistant managing director. Now he had only one. Matters came to a head over preparations for the next licence round of 1991, which the company had to win to remain in business. In 1989, Brum set up an application subcommittee chaired by himself, consisting of Alan Bremner, Desmond Smyth, John McCann and Jim Creagh. According to Alan Bremner, the first couple of meetings were 'absolutely shambolic'. 'Brum was ranting. He was seriously paranoid about the IBA, listing all the reasons why the company would not have its licence renewed.'

Now Desmond Smyth was losing faith, confiding to John McCann that this was not the way forward. Added to that, when Desmond came back from holiday that year, he had found Brum's attitude to him totally suffocating. There were over 150 memos from Brum waiting for his attention. Brum was certainly not conducting himself as a chairman. He was attempting to micromanage.

John McCann was now convinced that Brum was going to be difficult throughout the application process. While sitting on a beach on holiday, he decided that the management group simply had to find a way of moving him on for one very important reason – there was no chance of retaining the licence if he remained as chairman.

When John returned to work, Desmond had just gone on holiday, so John began canvassing the idea among trusted colleagues. John Hutchinson thought he was mad. 'Brum's the establishment. He is UTV. You cannot possibly take him on,' were his words. Alan Bremner agreed that Brum would have to go. The last of the trusted colleagues approached was Desmond. The only member of management not told at this stage was Jim Creagh, because they knew what his position would be.

Over the next six weeks or so, the dissidents, if we may call them that, met in various houses, planning how to proceed. Only one body could unseat Brum as chairman of the board and that was the board of UTV itself, so they decided to approach individual members and put their case. There was quite a big non-executive board and they had to get the timing right. Brum had a property in Florida and spent quite a lot of time there from about October on. He would fly home for board meetings. The dissidents calculated that once Brum was on the plane to Florida, it would take him a minimum of 36 hours to return to Northern Ireland. He would hear what was happening soon after landing, they imagined. So one Saturday, when they knew he was in the air, John McCann and Desmond went up to the North Antrim home of John McGuckian, who was vice-chairman, and told him what was afoot and their reasons for taking the action. They told him that they were going to see other members of the board to seek support. Over the next two days they worked their way around the board, except Captain Bill Henderson, Brum's brother, and found the members, as expected, very divided. In general terms, the old guard were pro-Brum, many believing that the only reason the company had won so many licence rounds lay in the person of Brum himself. Many, too, had a personal loyalty to him and were loath to see him removed in such a fashion from the company he had devoted his working life to.

When they approached Jim, he supported Brum. However, he did agree with the dissidents that Brum would have to keep a distance from the day-to-day running of the company. He could see the damage that the chairman's constant meddling was doing. It was an unhappy time for him: 'I became a pariah because I was not with them. It was a very lonely period for me as an executive director,' he remembers.

Jim Creagh tried to put a compromise package in place. Its main provision was that Brum remained in post, but expressly agreed to keep his hands off the day-to-day running of the company. He was also to nominate the time of his departure. Jim took two Brum-loyalist directors, Ann McCollum and Harry Catherwood, out to dinner and hammered out details of the compromise. But Brum would not agree to it, although his friend Jim believes to this day that he should have. The sticking point was the leaving date. He simply could not contemplate that day.

The board meeting to resolve the issue has been described by one insider as 'bloody'. During one of many recesses, one board member, John O'Driscoll, a stockbroker from Dublin, tried to put in place a compromise resolution, but by that stage McCann was against any deal. 'I knew that Brum could not have contained himself and he would have fought to oust us afterwards. He just had to go,' he says.

The board in reality had little choice but to go along with their executives. The company was on the cusp of a critical submission to the regulator against opposition to retain its licence. If they had voted for Brum, the top raft of executives would have left, either through resignation or through the subsequent bloodletting. Either way the licence submission, and therefore the company future, would be severely compromised. Furthermore, it could not have remained a secret that Brum had won such a battle and that in itself might have been sufficient grounds to deny UTV the licence, given the attitude of the IBA at the last licence round with regard to Brum's position.

The management team had won. The board vote went against Brum and he left in a way that no one, friend or foe, wanted to see. At his own wish, his departure was not marked by any festivities or celebration. He had been a good and faithful servant of UTV from its earliest days, a giant of a man, and when he fell, UTV shook.

Jim Creagh joined UTV almost at the start, in charge of presentation. He retired as deputy managing director and as a member of the board.

Chapter 9

UTV and animation

Ulster Television's first sustained use of animation was for its logo, the on-screen imagery which uniquely identifies the station and the company. The logo is important as an identifier and commerce is littered with famous, immediately recognisable logos. They come in many shapes and forms. Some, like that of Coca-Cola, are designs based on the words of the name itself; some are a mixture of a design and the name, like that of rival Pepsi. Some intermix the name with a design based on their initials, such as Rolls-Royce; some, like Gill & Macmillan, the publishers of this book, and the computer company Hewlett-Packard, use only their initials. (HP Sauce also uses just HP as a logo, but I have not heard that this causes confusion.) Some logos are so immediately recognisable that the design itself is enough to announce the company, the shell of Shell Oil being a good example. For oil companies, filling stations themselves could be regarded as rather large three-dimensional logos.

UTV's first identification logo.

In the world of television, logos are also known as idents – short for identification logos. The station's first on-screen logo was a pattern of seven dots joined together by six lines. Television as a moving picture medium begs for the company logos to be animated, and Ulster's logo was animated to a jingle based on the local tune, 'The Mountains of Mourne'. In the beginning there was endless fun speculation about what the dots meant. Some thought they represented the six counties, plus Belfast. Others said they represented the pattern of the main towns in Northern Ireland and that the dots could be superimposed on a map to demonstrate that. However, I don't think anybody got more than two dots to match up with towns or cities, with the rest on obscure townlands, halfway up mountains or in the sea. The truth was more prosaic. It was simply a graphical representation of the pattern made on the screen of an oscilloscope, and was the result of a public competition. Electronic engineers, including those in Ulster Television, needed oscilloscopes to measure and examine electrical signals. The original instruments used cathode ray tubes, just like those used in the original television sets. A dot, usually green, travelled across the screen in a wave pattern and that pattern had been translated by an artist into the UTV logo. The UTV logo was the only one in the ITV system that paid homage to the technology behind television.

Beyond the logo, animation was not on the shopping list of Ulster Television for a long time, not least because there were no local producers of animation. Secondly, animation is expensive because it is very labour intensive and very skilled work. Normally a moving picture requires the showing of twenty-five pictures or frames in a second in quick succession, though much animation makes do with twelve. But even at twelve frames per second, a quick calculation shows that 1 minute of screen action requires 720 frames. A 5-minute children's cartoon animation therefore needs over 35,000 frames.

Early animations consisted of simple drawings photographed one at a time. In 1906 in the United States, J. Stuart Blackton directed a 3-minute film entitled *Humorous Phases of Funny Faces*, where he drew comical faces on a blackboard and photographed them one at a time to make his film. This was called 'stop-motion' and the technique is the basis of all traditional animation. However, the cartoon which is generally regarded as the progenitor of all modern cartoons was

Steamboat Willie, the first Mickey Mouse sound cartoon, from the studios of Walt Disney. It was black and white, and the sound did not include dialogue, just music and effects. Both this and Blackton's film can been seen on the internet.

On the island of Ireland, substantial animation studios had to wait until the government in Dublin introduced tax incentives to encourage film-makers to invest. This led to the establishment of what might be called industrial animation, when companies such as Sullivan-Bluth set up shop. Sullivan-Bluth's move to Dublin in turn encouraged the setting up of other studios, and within a relatively short period of time, the policy of attracting animators led to three studios employing over 500 staff by 1990. It did not last though and within a relatively short time the animation bubble in Dublin burst. However, as a legacy, the Dublin area has a training infrastructure for animation in Ballyfermot College of Further Education and the Dun Laoghaire Institute of Art, Design and Technology.

One of those who emerged from the bubble was local animator, Alastair McIlwain, who began his career in London in the seventies as an animation director on commercials, television titles, series, shorts, promos and features. He has worked in the animation industry in the UK, Ireland and Europe since, using traditional and digital formats, winning BAFTA and RTS nominations and numerous awards for live-action shorts, commercials, title sequences and animated series in 2D and 3D. He was on the board of Northern Ireland Screen for six years and now exports his work from his production company, a partnership based in Holywood, Co. Down.

Holywood might claim to be the animation headquarters of Northern Ireland. When Alastair looks out his window, he can see close by the premises of Waddell Media, the company begun by Brian Waddell, who was the man in charge of Ulster Television programming for much of its early history. Within Waddell Media is Flickerpix, which began as a stand-alone animation company in east Belfast. They have been supplying Ulster Television with animation for some time. Their creative director and founder is Joel Simon, whose chosen path into animation production could scarcely have been more difficult. In fact, his experience to date, which includes being shot, is an unusual and inspirational tale of talent and persistence.

To begin with, Joel is a Belgian from the area of the Ardennes. The big advantage of living so near the German and Luxembourgish borders was that he grew up bilingual. (He is now trilingual through his excellent English.) English culture and language fascinated Joel from a young age, as did design, and eventually he ended up studying graphic design in Bolton. Whilst there, he came across a short piece of clay or plasticine animation of a parrot in a cage shot on Super 8 film. It interested him immediately and he wondered if he could do better. But Bolton College did not have animation on the syllabus.

Joel returned to Belgium for the summer break of two months and spent it trying animation, using a borrowed camera and working by instinct. He was captivated when he was able to project his work onto a wall and saw his characters move within the small theatrical set he had constructed. This first stab at animation, the same type as in the *Wallace and Gromit* films, lasted 2 minutes and had taken practically every free moment of the two-month break to make. On his return to Bolton, he showed the work to his tutor, who encouraged him to enter it in a student competition in Manchester. 'I remember sitting in the Corner House cinema in Manchester where about twenty student films were screened – with about twenty in the audience,' Joel says. 'When I saw people laughing at the points where I wanted them to, it was so re-affirming for me. The sensation of producing a response from an audience had never happened to me before. I had never considered film as a career but from that moment I was hooked.'

However, he admits he chose probably the single most difficult way to move from amateur to professional animation. He now knew what he wanted to do and the design course at Bolton had become of so little value that he did not deign to pick up the certificate of graduation. Instead, he rushed headlong into making another mistake by coming to Belfast to do a one-year top-up course in the summer of 1995. 'For me it was a disaster,' Joel says. 'The course was based on the history of art and design. Very theoretical and not at all what I wanted. I decided to drop out in the same week as I had joined. It meant I was in Belfast with no qualifications and penniless. I had to sign on the dole and knew no one here. I was living in a little flat with rowdy people so I had little sleep. This was my year zero.'

He decided that the only way out of this mess was to make a another film. The first step was to buy a sketch pad and then to write a film script. He borrowed a film camera (this was before cheap digital cameras were available), scrounged out-of-date film stock and began reading books about film-making. 'In those days all you really needed was a cine-camera, like the sixteen-millimetre Bolex I had. It was forty years old and worked like clockwork. I don't know of any piece of electronic equipment downstairs that I would have faith in operating forty years from now,' says Joel, smiling, because he has just remembered that the heart of the Bolex camera he was talking about was clockwork.

Flickerpix produced a series of animations to soundtracks provided by UTV, recorded in the make-up room prior to going on air. Here we see Paul Clark.

Joel set up Flickerpix, which consisted only of himself, and obtained a room to work in at Laganside studios in Belfast. Again, this was not the result of careful advance planning. 'Flickerpix came about by accident. I am not naturally a commercial person – I just want to make films,' he remembers. 'I was working at the time on my own in a windowless room on a claymation animated film called *Cyderpunks*, about middle-class teenagers living a down-and-out lifestyle in Belfast.'

As happens with erratic career paths, chance intervened. Brian Owens, head of presentation for UTV, happened to in Laganside studios on business. He was passing the room where Joel Simon was working, heard the music of a soundtrack and stuck his head in. 'He seemed quite intrigued at a Belgian animating clay characters in Belfast.'

143

By now it was 1997 and UTV was looking for something to enliven their Christmas season. Brian immediately thought that something like the clay characters he was looking at would be different and engaging. 'He asked me to come up with some characters for what were called 'stings', which were 15-second long mini-films for between programmes,' said Joel. 'Those stings were my first professional commission.'

Ten stings were needed, and he had only two months to come up with a concept and a script and make them. 'I did not have much time so I drew a bear and a dog, which is how Buska and Barney were born. The stings went down well with audiences. Everybody loved claymation those days because of Wallace and Gromit.'

Fate was to intervene yet again. After delivering the stings to UTV, Joel decided to spend Christmas in Kenya with his girlfriend, Jenny, now his wife. Two days before Christmas they both went on safari in a Land Rover, driving through a desert area with a missionary friend at the wheel. Suddenly a shot rang out. It was a bandit ambush. The driver of the Land Rover knew that if he stopped, it would be worse for all of them, so he slammed the accelerator to the floor and sped off. However, Joel had been shot in the leg and was losing a lot of blood. In fact, he almost died because of blood loss. Gangrene set in while he was in Kenya. It was decided to get him back to Belfast as soon as possible, not least because of the city's worldwide reputation for expertise in dealing with gunshot wounds. Unfortunately, it was too late to save his leg, which was amputated 10 centimetres above the knee. 'Between Christmas and New Year I was lying in a bed in the Royal Victoria when I turned over and saw Buska and Barney on television for the first time. I was on morphine, so my pleasure was heightened. Beside me was the *Belfast Telegraph* with the headline, "UTV man caught in an ambush." It was both glorious and tragic.'

The bullet did not damage the stiff backbone of Joel Simon. As might be surmised from the story of the first part of his life, he is not a person who buckles under adversity, not even when missing a leg. He recovered and threw himself once more into his work. One might say, his passion.

The meeting with Brian Owens was fortuitous, as was Owens's relationship with Alan Bremner, who was in charge of programmes at UTV. Owens had

Joel Simon beside his creation, Buska the Bear. Initially Joel's interests lay with animation, but puppetry is so much faster to produce. Buska is a big puppet and was suitably retired as commissionaire guard at the entrance to Flickerpix.

■ 'School Around the Corner' was a regular in the UTV schedules for a decade from 1995. It was a window into the lives of small children, the type of programme that has become a rarity in all television of late.

brought the original sting idea to Alan, who bought the idea on the spot and thereby set in motion the events that created Buska and Barney. Brian then developed the idea of using these characters for birthday greetings sent in by children. This was a successful means of interaction with an audience. A further development was to celebrate the millennium by having the cartoon characters ask children for drawings of the 'millennium bug'. As the millennium approached, there was speculation in the press that computers all over the world would malfunction because of early computer program design, which was in the habit of representing the year with two digits instead the full four. It was feared that on the turn of the century, the automatic dates embedded in these programs would come up with another date, resulting in the end of modernity, as some Armageddon reports were hinting. This was the feared 'millennium bug'. As it happened, UTV chose the correct way to deal with this approaching threat by getting Buska and

Barney to invite Northern Ireland children to send in drawings of the millennium bug. The station received over 2,000 bugs, which were displayed at Forestside Shopping Centre in south Belfast.

But the bug really did exist. Davy Sims was the producer of the Northern Ireland part of the BBC's website. He thought he would check and make sure all was well, from his Holywood home on New Year's Day. Moments later he was rubbing his post-celebratory eyes in disbelief. The date on the BBC site, for Northern Ireland and the world, was 1900.

A spin-off was the 'Groom Room'. Soundtracks were recorded in make-up in UTV with the station's main presenters and the audio was brought to Joel to create characters based upon the presenters for animated short films. 'I thought it was one of the best things we ever did in branding,' says Brian Owens. 'Everything about those shorts shouted UTV. And because we were just recording audio, we heard the presenters saying things that they would not say before a camera. It was super. We made a version for every presenter.'

Joel's small animation company was eventually bought by Waddell Media, of which it is now a part.

Robin McFarland joined Flickerpix in 2000. He too had something of a struggle to get into the business. He had studied English and art, and then taken a Higher National Diploma in management: 'What the HND taught me was that I did not want to push paper. The HND was training me for a life of feeling I didn't want to go to work.' So Robin went to Bangor Technical College and studied commercial sculpture, a course which was fashioned particularly for his needs. But when he emerged, his real difficulties began. He applied for jobs everywhere, including Japan, to no avail. Again, chance and luck played a part. Joel Simon's doctor was a family friend and this led to an introduction – and Robin got his foot on the first rung of the ladder as a freelance for Joel, principally model-making. Puppetry makes heavy use of sculpting skills.

There is a great deal of difference between stop-frame animation and puppetry. Animation is less forgiving. Robin explains why: 'When animating, all your sets, all your camera equipment, all the lighting has to be firmly fixed, ideally to a concrete floor, to eliminate vibration. All the joins need to be glued to prevent movement through heat expansion or cooling contraction. This meticulous preparation means that you can pick up a shot the next morning and be certain that everything is where it was when you took the last frame the day before. Otherwise, on film the join can be obvious.'

In animation, the rule of thumb is that you finish the shot or scene before downing tools, even if it means staying to midnight. This has to be done because, notwithstanding all precautions, something will change, and if you are in the middle of a scene, the change, however slight, will be immediately apparent. Even the aperture of the camera could be different the next day because the temperature of the studio might be different. 'With modern cameras which have automatic focus, you simply have to finish a shot,' declares Robin. 'The automatic focus will not do precisely the same thing the next day.'

And as if that was not sufficiently exasperating, the temperature and intensity of the lighting change as the day goes on: 'If you have had the lights on twelve hours the day before and come in in the morning, you will have a different quality of light. To the naked eye, it looks fine, but on tape you can see the difference when one shot is put against another.'

And then there is the unexpected to deal with: 'Quite frequently accidents happened. Hitting the camera or the lights is the easiest thing to do. You are in a confined space. You become so focused upon the models and what you are actually doing, and then without thinking, you take a step back and hit something. I don't think I know any animator who hasn't at some point done that. It can really mess things up because re-setting everything exactly as it was is practically impossible. If an accident like that occurs near the end of a shot, it is utterly infuriating. The air can be blue.' Robin pauses and almost shudders. Then he explains that there were ways around incidents like that, such as turning one shot into two, and zooming in or out. The production might by such means just lose two or three hours' work, but that is better than losing two or three days' work.

There are fewer such problems with puppetry. 'With stop motion, even if you are two thirds the way through your film, and you realise that it is not working, there is little you can do about it. You really only see the end result near the end,' Robin explains.

UTV were using Buska and Barney so much that Flickerpix pushed for a puppetry version. Robin outlines the advantages of changing from clay animation:

'A good day of shooting in stop motion will produce only eight seconds of material. With puppetry, we would be able to get a two-and-a-half-minute episode shot in a day, and probably some of the next day's episode as well. Also, there are often things in a script which look well on paper but do not work on the shoot. In puppetry you can instantly change. Changing in stop motion is much more difficult.' And of course this speed would be reflected in a reduced cost of production.

'Buska & Barney' was a pre-school puppetry series of fifteen episodes. It featured two good friends, Buska the bear and Barney the dog, who run a postal sorting office in space and are visited by funny aliens from time to time. So Robin made models of Buska and Barney. Buska the bear is large – a full-body puppet with room for somebody inside. The puppeteer needs to operate the head, the mouth and the arms, which calls for some compromises for humans with only two arms. This is how it is done. The puppeteer has one arm up, operating the head and mouth, and his or her other arm inside one of the puppet arms. So only one arm has full articulation. The other puppet arm is usually operated by a small loop of virtually invisible fishing line in such a way that, when one arm moves, so does the other to some degree, creating the illusion that both are being operated.

'If the other arm is needed for full operation, we usually have a second puppeteer who comes in from behind, wearing the second arm, which is fully detached from the main puppet,' says Robin. 'You need to be very careful with your camera angles to get this right, or the join shows!'

Barney is a glove-and-rod puppet, about the size of a small child. The puppeteer operates the head with a hand and there are two rods for the hand movements. There are replacement arms, which clip on and off with the kind of buckle you have on a bag. One is an arm which joins at the shoulder but with an opening at the elbow for the puppeteer's arm. Again, careful framing is needed. Only one person generally operates such a puppet.

Joel asked Robin then to design a 6-foot-diameter spaceship interior for Buska and Barney. Both men remember it as a lot of fun but hard work. 'There are no animation supplies in Northern Ireland, so you were always re-inventing the wheel,' says Robin. Then he adds, 'We built the spaceship on the floor and were operating while on mechanic's trolleys. With hindsight we ought to have raised it.

But then we had to find out much of this ourselves because nobody has written a manual.' To flatten the learning curve, Flickerpix engaged a puppeteer from the Jim Henson Company in London, an outfit which over the years has won over fifty Emmy awards and many Grammy awards. (Jim Henson was the creator of the Muppets, the rights to which are now owned by The Walt Disney Company.) They learnt a lot from the Jim Henson puppeteer.

The puppetry which grabbed the nation, seen on UTV screens, was 'Spitting Image', which ran from 1984 until 1996. The gloriously funny satirical latex puppets had a peak audience of eleven million, taking pot shots at celebrities, politicians and royalty. The creators, Roger Law and Peter Fluck, poured their anarchic ridicule on everybody they thought deserved it. But Fluck and Law had similar experiences to Flickerpix. Fluck invented a cheap brass-and-cable mechanism for manipulating eye movement. It was better than the £800 bespoke mechanism which could be bought in the film industry. He then miniaturised the eye mechanism, which was contained behind the bridge of the puppet nose. This in turn allowed the eyes to be made closer together to convey a really shifty look. But by doing that, he created another problem. The puppeteers had difficulty keeping their handholds – solved with another piece of low tech from Fluck, who bought fingerstalls for the puppeteers. It worked a treat. What's more, the fingerstalls were just the thing for modelling pitted flesh for characters such as Richard Ingrams.

As they gained experience, Law and Fluck found that the secret of a good caricature model was to get the shape of the head correct at the beginning. It helped if a character had a big mouth because this helped the puppeteer. In his highly entertaining autobiography, *Still Spitting at Sixty*, Roger Law wrote: 'The Queen's puppet benefited enormously from being based on a caricature with a big mouth, as did the Walter Matthau and Ian Paisley puppets.'

The editorial team at Central Television, who provided the programme for UTV and the network, were initially reticent about allowing 'Spitting Image' to mock the Queen, but as the series settled in, the royal family sketches became a regular feature. Roger Law said that the only 'Spitting Image' joke that was banned

■ The 'Spitting Image' puppet of Ian Paisley. The puppet is beside the puppet of (another) 'Barney', which was made for a UTV children's programme.

by the television regulator was a Bernard Levin sketch which had Levin's puppet explain that the reason he had become a writer was because he had been circumcised with a pencil sharpener.

Fluck and Law managed to keep almost 1,000 of their latex models intact and stored them for while in a warehouse in the east end of London. But storage costs money and Roger Law asked Sotheby's auction house to sell many of them. Margaret Thatcher went for £11,224, Mick Jagger for £7,645, the Queen for £4,383 and Prince Philip for £4,496. George Best went for £4,490, topping the list of sports personalities. He also went for more than the Blairs, who went for about £3,000 each.

In Holywood, Buska and Barney have survived, but their splendid spaceship interior with the sorting machinery was broken up. Sadly, Flickerpix could not afford the storage.

There are not many husband-and-wife teams on television, regional or network. Mike Nesbitt and Lynda Bryans shared the presenter's desk for news and current affairs programmes until Mike left in 2006. He was appointed a Commissioner for the Victims and Survivors of the Conflict in Northern Ireland. Lynda continued as one of the station's prime presenters.

Chapter 10

The day the UTV chairman thought the regulator might fire him

S ometimes broadcasting regulators grab hold of the wrong end of the stick and this episode is a good illustration. The ITC (Independent Television Commission), one of a series of regulators, was created by the 1990 Broadcasting Act to take over the functions of the small Cable Authority and more importantly the Independent Broadcasting Authority (IBA), itself the successor to the Independent Television Authority (ITA). Ofcom has been the regulator since December 2003. The original ITA lasted eighteen years; the IBA, which included independent radio in its remit, lasted seventeen years. The ITC lasted thirteen.

The framework of regulation needed to change more frequently in recent times to meet fast-changing conditions. The way we were receiving and using television began to alter very fast during the nineties. The old ITA and IBA regulators went about their business from 1955 to 1990 in a manner that is alien to the light-touch regulation we are now witnessing. The micro-management of what was being broadcast might seem incredible to twenty-first-century viewers, so it is worth looking at what once happened.

The old regulators, ITA and IBA, were at the heart of a self-supporting system. There was no income from the licence fee, which at the time of writing is all used to fund the BBC. As an aside, a classic example of a structure getting things wrong, because they cannot sort out the new technologies, is the UK TV licence fee. It is designed to provide income for a public service broadcaster, at the moment the BBC, but is cloaked in the obfuscation of legally needing a TV licence to watch or record television programmes as they are being shown, including UTV and all commercial and satellite channels. It makes no difference what you use. It could be a laptop, desktop computer, mobile phone, digital box, DVD recorder or a TV set – you still need a licence. Technically, therefore, you could be breaking the law if you do not already own a television licence and use a mobile phone capable of receiving live television over the internet. Quite a number of mobiles are capable of that.

This illustrates the point that regulation in a changing situation is difficult. Back in the fifties, it was a more certain world. The ITA and IBA had four main functions. First, they appointed the television companies to serve the various areas up and down the country, UTV included. These companies made their money by selling advertising and they in turn supported the regulator by paying a fee to cover the regulatory costs of administering the system and operating the transmitters. The companies were required to work within strict rules covering both programmes and advertising.

How did the ITA and IBA choose which company should be awarded the programme contract in each area? They looked at written submissions and then

In 1989 UTV transmitted a series of ten programmes about media skills, directed by Robert Lamrock, produced by Jamie Delargy and presented by Jacqui Berkley. The cartoon for the cover of the support material was by Blotski, aka Ian Knox, and might be considered a collector's item in itself.

interviewed directors. These contests were dubbed 'beauty contests' within the business. It was a subjective judgement. In the words of the IBA, 'Programme company contracts are awarded by the Authority to those applicants who in its view are likely to make the best contributions to the quality of Independent Broadcasting programme services.' Note that it was the Authority's view that prevailed. Nobody else's.

Once appointed, the ITV companies had other onerous regulatory burdens. Although the creative content of the individual companies was to be the responsibility of the companies themselves, the ITA and IBA supervised programme planning, 'to ensure that the output of the ITV services is of high quality and provides a proper balance of information, education and entertainment'. So each company decided on a quarterly programme plan in consultation with the regulator, who might want changes before giving approval. What the regulator was looking for at the planning stage was adherence to required specific periods of time allocated to certain types of programme, such as education, religion, news, documentaries and programmes for local interests and tastes. To help it define what local interests and tastes might be, the regulator maintained offices in the regions served by the companies, Belfast included. The regulator was looking for accuracy in news coverage and evidence of good taste. If something worried it, it could call for more detailed information about specific programmes in the projected schedules.

Again in the words of the IBA, 'The Authority's function is not merely regulatory but is closely involved in the positive processes of programme planning and the formulation of programme policy.' The ITA and IBA had no option but to adopt this proactive stance, because legislation made them answerable to Parliament and to the public for the content and quality of everything transmitted. The aim of Parliament was to achieve public service broadcasting, as defined by experience of the BBC's programming, while not interfering with artistic aims or the commercial independence of each company. Given that Members of Parliament have little time to watch television, except, of course, news and current affairs for the politics and for snippets of themselves, the wonderment is not that the system worked tolerably well in the first three decades of UK television, but that it worked at all.

Less controversially, the ITA and the IBA were the advertising standards regulators. For much of the early life of the system, no programme sponsorship was allowed because it was seen as blurring the distinction between programmes and advertising. Keeping the two emphatically separate was like canon law. Advertising had to follow a fat book of rules, which banned certain types of advertising, and limited advertising to 6 or 7 minutes per hour.

And finally, the regulator transmitted the programmes through transmitters it owned and operated. Areas like Wales and the Scottish highlands and parts of Northern Ireland were more expensive to serve with transmitters. Television transmitters, particularly the UHF 625-line ones which superseded the early 405-line VHF transmitters, were very much 'line of sight'. If hills got in the way of the signal, they caused a shadow and people living in the shadows got either a bad signal or none at all. So hilly areas needed more transmitters to fill in the shadows. A story circulating among IBA transmitter staff in the eighties related to one of the small 'filler' transmitters in Tyrone. It appeared that the signal had not proved strong enough and the height of the transmitting aerial would have to be raised by about a metre. A local planning officer was being consulted, because if possible, the IBA engineers wanted to dispense with the delays and paperwork of planning permission. But the planning officer dashed their hopes, saying that increasing the height of the structure would indeed need planning permission.

However, the official was particularly interested in the project, perhaps because of its novelty, but also perhaps because he would not be thanked by his own community if he needlessly delayed good television reception of UTV and other channels. Looking dubiously at the pinnacle of the structure, he asked eventually: 'As a matter of interest, how would you go about raising that aerial by three feet?'

'We wouldn't put it on top,' said the engineer. 'We would raise the base of the aerial and insert a metre section there.'

The planning officer nodded. 'In that case, since you are putting nothing on top, planning permission is not necessary.'

The IBA engineers left hurriedly before he could change his mind.

Programme regulation is the most public face of television regulation, but behind the scenes other types of regulation make their presence felt. One instance, which was largely hidden but which shook UTV, happened on the

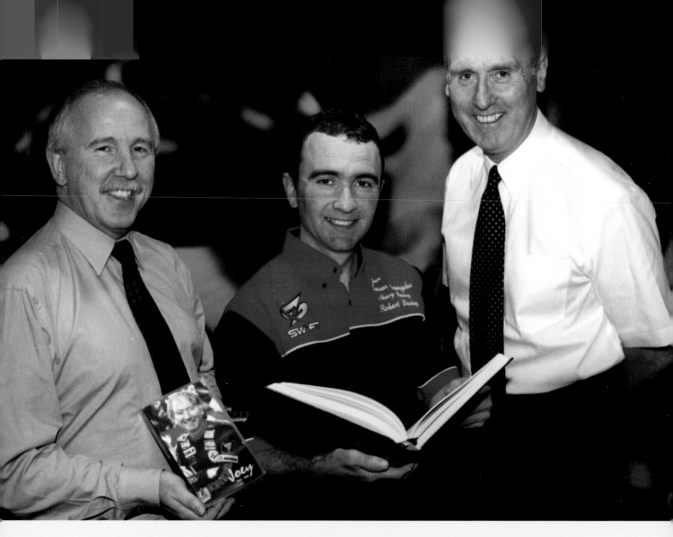

After motorcycle ace Joey Dunlop's death in 2000, UTV produced a video of his achievements. The profits of almost £80,000 went to his family. From the left, Maurice Goodwin, UTV operations manager, Robert Dunlop, Joey's brother and Alan Bremner, director of television. The book of memorial contained almost 100,000 expressions of sympathy. Robert himself was killed racing in 2008.

morning the Loyalist ceasefire was announced on Thursday 13 October 1994. By this time the regulator was the Independent Television Commission.

At the time, this day was believed to be the one on which peace was finally to come to Northern Ireland. History and hindsight now inform us that this was not the day which brought final peace. The greatest single incident of carnage in the Troubles was still to happen, the Omagh bomb. But the war-weary people of Northern Ireland thought they were experiencing the end of the Troubles. Seven weeks before, the IRA had declared a ceasefire, and now the three main Loyalist paramilitary groups were announcing a ceasefire in Belfast. A statement by the Combined Loyalist Military Command, an umbrella group for the Ulster Volunteer Force, the Ulster Defence Association and the Red Hand Commando, was read by Gusty Spence, a convicted terrorist who had been sentenced to twenty years in 1966 for killing a Catholic barman.

Gusty Spence said that the command would 'universally cease all operational hostilities as from 12 midnight on Thursday 13 October 1994,' a statement loudly welcomed by political leaders, from Unionists to Sinn Féin's Gerry Adams. The Taoiseach, Albert Reynolds, said the announcement marked the 'closure of a tragic chapter in our history'. The Prime Minister, John Major, described the truce as 'another very important part of the jigsaw falling into place'. The Loyalist paramilitary organisations had killed over 900 people in twenty-five years, and more than 3,000 people had died overall.

Inside UTV, there was a feeling in the newsroom that it had not covered the IRA ceasefire as well as it could have done. Rob Morrison, the head of news and current affairs, felt this particularly. On the morning of the Loyalist ceasefire, Alan Bremner got a call from Rob telling him that Ivan Little was on his way to a press conference. Rob was particularly pleased to have had early warning of this unusually early news conference. It was happening before nine o'clock. UTV's first bulletin was to be at 9.30 a.m., when the station went on air. UTV shared channel 3 with GMTV, the television company in London which had the franchise for the breakfast period. To complicate matters further, UTV contributed to the GMTV news bulletin at nine o'clock with an insert about the weather, but there was no news content from Belfast. The airtime at this point of the day belonged to GMTV.

Alan Bremner asked how GMTV were covering the important ceasefire announcement and, to the amazement of both Rob and Bremner, found that GMTV was going to ignore it. In that newsroom in London, the significance of the Loyalist ceasefire was neither perceived nor understood. In mitigation, the thrust of the GMTV breakfast was light-hearted tabloid material. It was not a news channel and made no secret of the fact that its programme priorities lay elsewhere. GMTV expected that the breakfast audience that wanted a news and current affairs programme would be tuned to BBC.

This was the backdrop to what would be one of UTV's worst days in its history of relationships with a regulator.

Alan Bremner was competitive. He did not want it said that the ITV system handed a news scoop over to the BBC because a GMTV news editor was ignorant of the fact that there was more than one paramilitary organisation fighting in Northern Ireland. He picked up a telephone and spoke to the transmission controllers of GMTV and had it confirmed that they would be ignoring the Loyalist ceasefire. Bremner then said that the circumstances were exceptional, so exceptional that he wanted to leave the nine o'clock GMTV news bulletin before it ended and just ahead of the UTV weather insert. In that space they could broadcast a short report about the ceasefire as a preface to the weather, which came from UTV's studios. He remembers that the conversation wandered a bit. GMTV and UTV were both in uncharted waters. The GMTV people said that this had never been done before and wondered if it was technically feasible. Bremner said that it was. His impression at that point was that the GMTV staff were happy enough to go along with this.

However, Bremner was talking to relatively junior staff at GMTV in London. He admits he did not manage to talk to GMTV's programme controller, though he did try to. Furthermore, he did not have the authority to truncate GMTV's own news bulletin. And remember, the airtime at nine o'clock belonged to GMTV, not to UTV.

Alan Bremner, nevertheless, in the heat of the moment and in response to the pressure of the importance of the news item, broke into GMTV's airtime with a report from Ivan Little on the Loyalist ceasefire at around nine o'clock. After that, things began to unravel, as far as Bremner was concerned.

When John McCann, general manager, came in at about 9.15 a.m., Bremner told him that he might have done something to cause problems. Bob McCourt, the chief engineer, came in and said, 'We did not have any right to trespass onto GMTV airtime.' John McCann felt the same as Bremner, that no matter what the rules and regulations said, it had been important to transmit this most important news to the audience in Northern Ireland. He did not want ITV to be denigrated because GMTV had no word of it. John McCann then reported the events to Desmond Smyth, the managing director, who was not happy.

Desmond then briefed the chairman and reported to his management team that the top man in the company was not inclined to be difficult about this. The general view among management was that Bremner had made a technical mistake, but for the right reasons. John McCann was particularly of this view and this had the effect of stiffening management resolve to wrap the protection of the company round Bremner. In the meantime, Bremner had to apologise to the board and his management colleagues.

Student notes for the 'Understanding Northern Ireland' series of 1992, produced by UTV for ITV broadcasts to schools throughout the UK. The producer was John Scobbie, the writer Jonathan Bardon.

As it happened, the ITC was shortly afterwards conducting a meeting in its Belfast office. The ITC chairman was Sir George Russell, a businessman from the north-east of England, who was taking a very hard line with UTV. The local ITC commission member at the time was Professor Seán Fulton, a distinguished academic in the field of education at Queen's University. He was more sanguine about the episode, and when he had talked to Bremner and told him that while the ITC would regard what had happened as a clear breach of the licence, he personally understood why it had happened. On their visit to Belfast the Commission members were scheduled to visit Havelock, a visit Alan Bremner was not looking forward to: 'I was pretty nervous. I remember George Russell walking into the building with a look of determination. He was not in a good mood.'

At UTV, Sir George had taken John McGuckian into an office for a private word. Sir George told him forcefully that he believed the company had been guilty of an act of airwave piracy. The ITC had yet to deliver its formal verdict, but the UTV chairman was left in no doubt that serious consequences could be expected.

The UTV visit came to an end and the hosting management party broke up. Bremner was by now feeling extremely uncomfortable and apologised again to his chairman: 'It could be you or me, as far as our jobs are concerned.'

Later the ITC commission members met in formal session in their offices in Upper Queen Street in Belfast and considered the fate of UTV. At the time I was the ITC Officer for Northern Ireland and was asked for a report. I had not known what had happened at UTV but I could see that Sir George was in a thunderous mood and was influencing those at the meeting to come down hard on the company. I had decided to fight the corner of UTV. My position was delicate, in that I was supposed to be dispassionate and detached in my approach, as befitted an officer of the regulator. I also was aware that some in the room would be aware that I had known Alan Bremner for years, from before he had joined UTV, and that my motivation could on that basis be called into question. To that degree, I was putting myself in the firing line, but given my genuinely held interpretation of events, I could see no other option.

The faces around the long table turned to me. I began by showing the commissioners, who came from all over the UK, the front page of one of the local newspapers. Across the top in huge letters, easily visible to the end of the room, were two words: 'IT'S OVER.'

I took a deep breath and began. 'Look at that headline. It is a headline many of us in Northern Ireland despaired of ever seeing. There is scarcely a family that has not been touched, often torn apart, by the violence over a quarter of a century in a conflict that had been grabbing headlines in practically every country in the world. It wasn't over when the IRA declared their ceasefire some six or seven weeks ago and all of us here knew that. The Loyalists, armed to the teeth, were still out there and still ready to fight, because they did not believe in the IRA ceasefire. Many were worried that if the Loyalists did not come on board, the IRA ceasefire might not hold.'

I told them that there were those on the Republican side who were very hesitant about laying down arms while the Loyalist paramilitary organisations were not stepping down. In that situation, the IRA ceasefire, which was brittle, could crumble if Loyalists mounted an attack, or if dissident Republicans did the same because there had been no positive reaction to the IRA move.

'In those circumstances, when that Loyalist ceasefire was announced, it was the duty of every broadcaster to get the news of it out on the streets as fast as possible. It would have been yet another tragedy if an attack had been mounted because news of the final ceasefire was delayed, merely to keep to licence condition. Releasing the news as fast as possible, particularly in this very strong channel 3 area, was in my view a matter transcending trivial licence conditions. This incident would have been unthinkable in East Anglia or Yorkshire: it had happened because of Northern Ireland. Those very serious considerations must affect our view of what the company did. Bremner broke the rules but he was protecting the integrity and news credibility of the ITV system.'

Professor Fulton was sympathetic to what I was saying. So were some other commissioners, and in the end Sir George's anger moderated. UTV had its knuckles rapped and Bremner, half seriously, was told to stay out of Havelock House until after 9.30 a.m. (when GMTV went off air). GMTV's role in the affair was not seriously examined by the ITC. When a senior UTV executive had phoned to say that this very important story should have been part of their nine o'clock bulletin that morning – a most unusual if not unique intervention – someone in GMTV ought to have asked why it was not. Later in the day, GMTV would have become aware of the story because it was headlines for the rest of the day. But then, not being up to speed on Northern Ireland events was never a regulatory matter.

'It was the worst three months of my career,' said Bremner afterwards.

Chapter 11

John McCann, UTV group managing director.

The battle to remain independent

O ne of the key elements and, from a regional point of view, one of the most valuable attributes of the original federal structure of the independent system was the notion that regional television was sufficiently important to have the whole country participating, not just the south-east of England. The ITA (Independent Television Authority) and its first chairman, Kenneth Clarke, had as one of their aims shifting some of the driving force behind the new medium of television out of London and into the country at large.

In time, the ITA became the IBA and in a review of the first twenty-one years of the system, was very explicit about the philosophy of the founders of the system:

> The Authority has preferred a diversified and multiple control of programme companies to a concentrated or single ownership, and has further preferred that regional and local companies should contain strong local participation. This is a reflection of the Authority's policy of seeking to shape the institutions of Independent Broadcasting in such a way as to increase the diversity and number of the nation's means of communication . . . Generally, in its selection of companies, the Authority has sought to provide a broad balance of interests within the system as a whole and to ensure that the control and ownership of each company forms an identity and character likely to provide a balanced and high quality service and genuinely reflect the area served.

Undoubtedly this led to a slightly odd and somewhat divided ITV. Since most of the ITV companies were outside London, there was a palpable thread of anti-metropolitan and anti-centrist ethos inbuilt within the system, but nevertheless significant programmes within the network schedule were provided from London and the southeast. Left to their own devices, London was too big a draw for companies and their producers to ignore. For example, ATV (later Central), the company serving the English midlands, maintained studios at Elstree, close to London, until the IBA forced a change.

Though the strategic and commercial decisions may have been made in the capital, editorial decisions were made locally. ITV's developing personality incorporated an independent spirit and provided a rich seam of regional talent. In the mid-1950s, this was not what BBC television was doing. Its heart was in London, and perhaps its soul too.

The original good intentions of the ITA and IBA worked well, but were destroyed by politicians, specifically in the 1990 Broadcasting Act. The federation of individual programme companies was progressively demolished from that time. The beginning of the end of the old federal structure might be seen in the merger of Yorkshire Television and Tyne Tees Television in 1992. Yorkshire was one of the biggest television companies and Tyne Tees was much smaller, so it was more of a takeover than a merger. The franchises remained separate, but this takeover could be seen as the first step in the creation of ITV plc, which would eventually own all the franchises to broadcast in England and Wales. In 1994 the regulation of ownership of ITV franchises was relaxed, to make it possible for one company to own two ITV licences outside London. So Carlton bought Central, Meridian bought Anglia and Granada took over LWT (London Weekend Television). The 1996 Broadcasting Act hammered the final nails into the coffin of the old idea of separate television companies standing alone to serve their individual communities and combining to provide a network.

Carlton also took over Westcountry and a consultation between the competition regulator and the Department of Trade cleared the way for the merger of the two giants of accumulated ITV companies, Granada and Carlton – although this did not take place until 2004, when the two combined to form ITV plc. The federal structure had now disappeared almost without trace. ITV plc now owned Anglia (central and eastern England), Border (border region between England and Scotland), Carlton (London weekday), Central (east and west Midlands), Granada (north of England), HTV (Wales and west of England), London Weekend Television (London weekends), Meridian (south and south-east England), Tyne Tees (north-east England), Westcountry (south-west of England), and Yorkshire (Yorkshire).

Outside ITV plc lay the Scottish Media Group, owning Scottish Television (centred in Glasgow) and Grampian in Aberdeen, which Scottish Television bought in 1997. Channel Television in the Channel islands remained independent, partly because the Channel Islands are not part of the United Kingdom and partly because the company is very small – easily the smallest in the network. Also outside ITV plc, of course, is UTV.

While ITV was coalescing, UTV was steadfastly remaining true to the vision of the founding fathers and asserting its individuality. The company increased its local programming through the nineties, dramatically pulling away from the network in terms of audience share. The audience at large would not have noticed the increased share, but the company did its best to point to the achievement. A good example was 1993, a year of expansion in local programme output. In that year,

UTV provided over 600 hours of regional programmes, an increase of almost 90 hours compared with 1992. The ITC review of 1993 regional programmes affirmed that UTV had met and in most cases exceeded the programme targets it had undertaken and that that it had commissioned more than the statutory minimum of 25 per cent of its regional output from independent programme-makers. The company itself declared:

> In 1993 UTV was proportionately the most viewed television channel in the United Kingdom. Research indicates that this popularity depends greatly on the strength of our regional programmes, which attract 17% more viewership than the average across the whole of ITV. This success is built on the talents and expertise of our programme makers, but also reflects effective application of extensive programme research into viewers' needs and preferences. This research provides us with pro-active information about audience interests and availability, as well as in-depth analysis of programme performance. It makes an important contribution to shaping a regional programme service which is interesting and attractive to our viewers.

The strength of local programming was what was setting UTV apart from the big English stations which formed the backbone of the network. Local programmes were not all that popular in places like Birmingham, Manchester, Leeds or London. In large conurbations where local identity was being changed by social and economic conditions, by population movement and immigration, the appeal of local programming was shown to be limited. Broadly, the further north and west you went from London, the more local programming appealed to audiences.

Identity, particularly local identity, was very important for Ulster Television, important enough for there to be arguments internally about whether the station was called UTV or Ulster Television. When Brum Henderson was in post, it was always to be Ulster Television. He abhorred the acronym and admonished anyone in the building he heard using it, just as there once were managers in the BBC who blew a gasket if they heard anyone refer to the organisation as 'the Beeb'.

UTV was married to colloquialism. John McCann realised that the company had made its fortune by being completely comfortable with the vernacular. 'We moved away from the split brand personality of UTV/Ulster Television,' he says. 'When I came I was told, "You must always say 'Ulster Television'." And on screen our announcers were saying, "Ulster Television" but if you picked up the *Belfast Telegraph*, *Irish News* or even Brum's brother's newspaper, the *News Letter*, it was writing about UTV. So when Brum moved on, we rebranded as UTV and were able to use the "UTV – is your TV"!'

Julian Simmons, personality presenter at UTV.

While speaking to me in his office, John looks out the window: 'If you could make television for that street out there, everybody in that street would watch it. You can't, because the economics won't work. But if you can get across the message to all the streets that you are their local television station, then people are much more likely to watch. Of course, the programmes still have to be right; they have to be good.'

That's when viewers saw a change in the on-screen presence of the station, hammering the localness of UTV. To that end, the company deleted as much reference on-screen to ITV as it could. It took the ITV promos (programme promotions or trailers) and rebranded them UTV. UTV was shouting, 'Local, local'. UTV continued as the only company with on-screen continuity because it believed, and Alan Bremner, the man in charge of local programming at the time, believed, that people here liked it. It chose people like Julian Simmons, who could really engage with the viewer – people loved the camp presence. As so often happens, Julian's role emerged by chance. He was a part-time announcer and newsreader at the station while not at his day job at Air Canada. His announcing was straight until one Christmas. In his own words, it happened thus: 'Continuity was very straight . . . and then one Christmas, I was in for four or five days over the Christmas period, all done up like a dog's dinner and a dickie bow . . . no news to read, so I started introducing

■ John B. McGuckian, Chairman, UTV Media.

these programmes and acting a "bit of the lig" in between the programmes. And it went down very well, apparently. They decided I would do weekends permanently: Friday/Saturday/Sunday primetime, where the programmes are all entertainment: nothing hard or heavy.' Though he might shudder at the thought, Julian is now something of an institution, having assumed in some measure the mantle of James Young, the much loved camp entertainer of former years.

But heavy local identity and the performances of Julian were scant protection from company predators. How did UTV manage to escape being swallowed up by another media group? By the skin of its teeth, as the following account of a very serious takeover attempt demonstrates.

At the end of the summer in 1997, Scottish Television made what is known in the world of finance as a 'dawn raid' on UTV's shares, quickly buying up 14.9 per cent of the company. There are stock exchange rules for this kind of game. Under those rules, a buyer can only take 14.9 per cent, and then must wait a wait a week, after which he or she could buy another 10 per cent. The buyer must then wait a further week before going to 29.9 per cent and is then free to launch a full bid. John McCann, UTV's general manager, was in little doubt that Scottish Television was making a serious attempt to swallow UTV, just as they had done to Grampian earlier in the year.

John McCann remembers: 'That was a very interesting period. Scottish were offering around two pounds a share and we thought we could offer a much better deal for our shareholders than the Scottish bid. However, there was also feeling at senior levels within UTV that this could be the end of the line for us as an independent company.'

Desmond Smyth was not at his desk at the time because he was unwell. Because the circumstances were pressing, John McCann and the company Chairman, John B. McGuckian, went to Desmond's house to see if there was anything that could be done to prevent the Scottish takeover. Desmond told them he believed that the Scottish bid would by this stage be difficult to thwart. But John McCann was not yet ready to concede. He realised that Scottish was doing its best to keep itself from being swallowed by the monolith of ITV plc and expansion was one way of making a company more indigestible. In their place, he would probably have tried the same tactic.

However, UTV still had a little time for manoeuvre, though not much space. Many at management and board level were agreeing with Desmond, that coming up with a plan of resistance in the space of a week was a tall order. In a week Scottish could begin buying more UTV shares.

A company response of some kind was required and therefore a special meeting of the board was called. It took place the day before the week was up. Early that morning, John McCann came to see Desmond, who had by now returned to work. The trouble was that right at that moment, McCann did not know what weapons the company could use, but he did believe that the first stage was to secure a decision to resist, then to work out what to do. It should be remembered that at the time 'takeover fever' was raging through the television industry and no targeted company had successfully beaten off an attack. Hence the depressed mood at Havelock House. However, before the board meeting started, the management group had made the strategic decision to fight the bid by whatever means possible.

At the meeting three representatives from the company's London brokers, Dresdner Kleinwort Benson, who had been invited for this crucial meeting, were seated beside the chairman. The main broker looked every inch the City type, expensively and conservatively attired, almost archetypally upper crust English in appearance and manner.

The debate among board members began with tossing ideas about, trying to think of something to see off Scottish Television. Bremner was a relatively new member of the board and was unsure of what to expect of a meeting like this. The non-executive directors were JB McGuckian in the chair, the Earl of Antrim, Roy Bailie, Roland Benner, Helen McClure, Lady McCollum and John O'Driscoll.

Alongside the non-executive directors were the executive directors, Desmond Smyth, the managing director, John McCann, general manager and Alan Bremner, with John Rooney in attendance as company secretary.

'What if we directors started to buy shares?' somebody asked. Such a move would soak up the available shares on the market. But there was a snag. The brokers and others advised that directors could not do that because the company was in a 'closed period' – i.e., it had not announced its half-year results and, by

Presenters Pamela Ballantine and Frank Mitchell.

stock market rules, no directors could deal in shares until those results were public. The half-year results were not due to be released for another two weeks.

Joe Mahon, presenter, producer and director of 'Lesser Spotted Ulster'.

John McCann then countered, 'Why don't we bring forward the meeting approving the half-yearly results? We could set up a special meeting now and have the accounts passed speedily. We would therefore be into a new period and then we could buy shares as a defence and as a measure of confidence. That would drive up the share price and wrong-foot the Scottish bid price.' With that, John McCann and Desmond Smyth left the meeting to study with maximum haste what could be possible along these lines. They probably thought there would be a break in the meeting before the chairman asked about who was to buy what shares.

The events were taking the UTV brokers from London far away from their comfort zones. They gave the appearance of never having encountered a situation like this in their professional lives. Meanwhile Alan Bremner remained at the table, now the only executive director present. In his head reverberated the phrase, 'directors to buy shares'. He already had some shares in UTV and no financial reserves except what was in his current account and his savings account. 'On the assumption that it is within the rules, we'd better decide how much we are going to buy,' continued the chairman.

The non-executive directors began coming up with figures. The chairman himself came up with a few million. 'I thought they were talking sterling because the shares were about two pounds apiece,' says Bremner. 'It came round to me and I could scarcely find a voice to say, "Ten thousand."'

'Shares?' asked the chairman.

Bremner replied hoarsely that he thought people round the table were talking cash. John B. said, 'No. It's shares.' Bremner nodded weakly, his savings book bursting into flames inside his head.

John and Desmond returned to the room, and at this point the chairman dismissed the brokers and moved to the next business.

When John McCann had left the meeting he talked to a partner in the accountancy firm which handled the UTV audit. The partner came over to Havelock House and McCann immediately got the company accounts signed off. That was the first stage. Normally the statement from the company chairman accompanying the financial statement is a carefully crafted piece of prose, taking days to emerge from multiple drafts. This statement for the chairman was produced in 20 minutes, from start to final copy. John B. McGuckian read it, approved it and signed. And that took the company out of the closed period.

So the following morning the directors were able to buy the shares. This had two effects. First, it declared publicly to shareholders that the directors had confidence in the company and its present ownership. And secondly it soaked up the available shares. Scottish managed to gain another 2 or 3 per cent, but that was their lot. A few months later Scottish Television finally signalled defeat by selling their 18 per cent of UTV shares to the Canadian company CanWest.

But the day was saved and UTV breathed a sigh of relief.

This was not quite the end of the story. UTV subsequently explored the possibility of merging with SMG, which owned not only the two Scottish ITV franchises but also Virgin Radio, a national radio service. However, by the end of February 2007 there had not been enough progress and the proposal lapsed. Thus UTV remained in control of its own destiny.

Chapter 12

Governments and UTV journalism

Right from the beginning there has been a tension between the governments and the media over coverage of the Troubles. There are not many television stations that can claim to have indirectly helped bring down a government. It is not a claim that UTV is anxious to press or even acknowledge, but nevertheless, the programme 'Suffer Little Children' played a part in bringing down the Dublin government of Albert Reynolds. It was broadcast in the 'Counterpoint' current affairs series on 6 October 1994. The reporter, Chris Moore, uncovered two intertwined strands of a malevolent story in the one programme and the effects were devastating both politically and religiously.

The first story was a forty-year catalogue of child-molestation by a Northern Ireland Catholic priest of the Norbertine Order, Brendan Smyth, who used his privileged pastoral position to get access to his victims. He assaulted hundreds of children in numerous parishes throughout Ireland and the United States in a brutal betrayal of trust.

The second strand told of the other betrayal, that of a Church which had known of this man's criminal predilections and activities for decades and dealt with it by moving him from parish to parish, while remaining silent about why their employee was being moved. In some cases, the Order did not inform the diocesan bishop that Smyth had a history of sexual abuse and should be kept away from children. This resulted in yet more children suffering.

The programme was an old-fashioned scoop whose ramifications ricocheted internationally. Metaphorically, packs of hunting hounds were let loose on the Church, seeking out child-molesters wherever they were to be found, discovering more wrongdoing and sending the institution into a state of disarray. In the resulting loss of respect and prestige, congregations fell and the number of men electing to be priests reduced considerably. It was probably the worst calamity to hit the Western Church in half a millennium.

That in itself did not have a direct political effect. What caused the political damage was the incompetent handling by the Attorney General's office in Dublin of an extradition request from the police in Northern Ireland. This led to a delay of some months in Smyth facing trial. The coalition government of Fianna Fáil and Labour collapsed under the strain. The resignation statement of the Taoiseach, Albert Reynolds, made plain the connection with the Brendan Smyth affair: 'In the circumstances that have led to this decision, I simply wish to state that it was never, never my intention to mislead the Dáil or withhold any material information from it. I sought a deeper investigation of the circumstances surrounding the handling of the Father Brendan Smyth extradition case from the new Attorney General and have been prepared to draw the appropriate conclusions without flinching.'

And so ended the premiership of a man whom history may judge to have laid much of the groundwork that led to peace in Northern Ireland through his decision to work closely with the British prime minister, John Major. But that is how politics can unfold, how history unfolds and, in this case, how good journalism can unfold.

The following year a sequel on the same subject was aired.

The competent journalism was no accident. Chris Moore as reporter was a leading light in the 'Counterpoint' team, working under the editorship of Michael Beattie. The full team was Tony Curry, Michael Nesbitt, Paul Robinson, Ken Devlin, Mary Curry and production secretary, Mary McCleave. I first met Michael Beattie as a young reporter back in the mid-seventies. I was Downtown Radio's inaugural programme controller and Beattie was recruited to his first broadcasting job as a journalist in the Downtown newsroom. He was good, and therefore he was quickly on the move. He went to UTV within ten months and learnt about television under an excellent producer, Rory Fitzpatrick, working on the lunchtime magazine. He moved into UTV's newsroom under editor Robin Walsh and even this early in his career presented 'UTV Reports' for a time, when David Dunseith was ill. When Robin went to BBC, Beattie took a cut in salary to follow him. On hearing this, UTV's droll newsreader Brian Baird said to him, 'Dear boy. The BBC is a wonderful institution. But who'd want to live in an institution?'

Spoken in jest, but the grain of truth was there. In 1980 Beattie was back in UTV as deputy to news editor Colm McWilliams, another journalist for whom colleagues had a high regard. When Gloria started with 'Good Evening Ulster' in 1979, Michael Beattie became editor. This was UTV's flagship programme for the next three years until Gloria left to go to London. In the meantime, Derek Murray who was working under Brian Waddell, started 'Counterpoint' in the early eighties, and Beattie was appointed editor. In the beginning there were just three people: Beattie, Brian Black as presenter and Jamie Delargie as researcher. Beattie remembers it as a 'fabulous period'.

'The year away in the BBC had opened my eyes. I had worked in London for three weeks at a time with Billy Flackes and seen more of the London influence. UTV tended to be a place where everybody had always worked in UTV. Derek Murray was happy for me to bring in freelance directors from outside, so I got directors who had worked throughout the ITV system. I think this added a lot, for me and for UTV generally.' It was a very productive but exhausting period. Beattie remembers the timetable thus: 'Filming Monday and Tuesday, editing Wednesday

and Thursday, and transmission that Thursday night. Then start panicking about next week. The three of us were churning it out from September to June with breaks at Christmas and Easter. It was really tough, but we loved it and had great fun doing it.'

Between 1985 and 1987 Beattie left to work as an independent producer with David Barker, who set up one of the first television facility and production houses in Belfast. It was here our paths crossed again. I was an independent producer at the time and together Michael and I made a six-part series about industry for the BBC. When Derek Murray left UTV, Beattie returned there for the second time and became, alongside Andy Crockart, a deputy to Brian Waddell. He was now in charge of UTV's factual programming, including news.

A significant programme made the year before 'Suffer Little Children' was the 'Counterpoint' on the tenth anniversary of the Maze Escape. In the biggest British prison escape, thirty-eight IRA prisoners escaped in September 1983 from H-Block 7. One prison officer died of a heart attack and twenty others were injured, including two shot with smuggled handguns. Programmes like this are always controversial. Before a single step is made in their production, a large number of viewers object to the subject matter being treated at all.

In this programme, Beattie was having a problem with what was known as the broadcasting ban. In October 1988, the Government announced that organisations in Northern Ireland believed to support terrorism would be banned from directly broadcasting on the airwaves. The ban affected eleven Loyalist and Republican organisations but Sinn Féin, the political wing of the IRA, was the main target. The ban was prompted partly by what had been happening in the period leading up to its sudden announcement, and partly by the fact that the Republic had operated a similar ban since the early seventies. In 1987 there had been the killing of eight IRA attackers on Loughgall police station, along with a passer-by, the thwarting of an attack on the English home of Secretary of State Tom King, and the killing of eleven people and injuring of sixty-three at a cenotaph ceremony at Enniskillen. 1988 saw the killing of three IRA members in Gibraltar and then the extraordinary attack by Michael Stone on mourners at their funerals in Belfast, killing three more people. The next day, two Army corporals who had mistakenly driven near the funeral procession of an IRA man shot by the Army were taken from their car, stripped, beaten and killed. Added to the rest of the violence, it was altogether a particularly bad period in the Troubles.

What probably stuck in the gullet of government was the broadcasting in April 1988 of a Thames Television documentary on ITV – and therefore also on UTV – called 'Death on the Rock', in which witnesses said that two of the Gibraltar three had been shot trying to surrender, the third had been shot in the back and all three had been killed at point blank range. The foreign secretary, Sir Geoffrey Howe, had described the decision by the IBA to allow the programme as 'irresponsible'.

Clearly, there was a strong feeling among ministers that something had to be done to stop Sinn Féin using the media to justify and defend the actions of the IRA. The broadcasters bridled at this restriction and began using actors. It meant that instead of hearing, say, a Sinn Féin spokesperson, viewers and listeners would hear an actor's voice reading a transcript of the Sinn Féin person's words.

The ban had some bizarre effects. For example, at the BBC, veteran reporter Peter Taylor had made a film about the Maze prison, featuring Loyalist and Republican prisoners. The restrictions allowed Taylor to interview prisoners in their personal capacity without resorting to actor voices, because they were deemed not to be representing a restricted organisation in their personal capacity. However, Taylor was required to use an actor voiceover when the IRA's spokesman for food was complaining about the size of the sausage rolls.

Beattie was not in the remotest sense an apologist for the IRA, but he found the broadcasting ban getting in the way of his making a sensible programme about the escape. 'We decided we were going to use the IRA people who had escaped,' Beattie says. 'We were going to interview them, and use their words. Again, I was given a free hand to make the decisions about "Counterpoint" by UTV management. I studied the legislation in great detail. One was not to broadcast the direct speech of those representing or purporting to represent a list of organisations, or the words of those speaking in favour of or in support of those organisations.'

Chris Moore and Beattie conducted the escapee interviews in Dublin at the Killiney Court Hotel and somehow the Northern Ireland Office got to hear of this. 'I don't recall how the NIO even knew we were making this programme,' Beattie says. 'I certainly hadn't told anyone at Stormont. They had also discovered that I was intending to use their direct speech and that's even more mysterious. Again, I don't know how they found this out. I then got a call late one night, advising me that this would be a very foolish course of action.'

Beattie used a novel stratagem against the NIO. The programme had also interviewed Sir James Hennessy KBE CMG, the Chief Inspector of Prisons for England and Wales, who had conducted the inquiry into the Maze escape. In his report into the escape, Sir James had concluded that only 'inhuman and unacceptable methods' could guarantee absolute security. He also said the escape was a matter for some congratulation for the Republican movement. With these words, Beattie concluded that within the strict meaning of the broadcasting ban, this senior establishment figure could be interpreted as speaking in support of a

Gerry Kelly fronted 'Kelly's People', a short series which was a precursor of the 'Kelly' show, which ran for a remarkable seventeen years.

listed organisation. On that basis, he informed the NIO that if he was to be forced to actor or subtitle the escapees, then he was going to do the same with Sir James Hennessy. With that, nothing more was heard from the NIO and the programme went out without actor voices. The restrictions were finally lifted in 1994, following the announcement by the IRA of a ceasefire. The Government was probably quietly relieved to be rid of the measure since it had never worked as intended.

'Counterpoint' won three Celtic Film Festival awards in a row for the Maze programme, the Brendan Smyth programme and its sequel. The team also won several Entertainment and Media Awards (EMAs) and several IPR media awards. Michael Beattie, following a well-trodden path, left UTV in 2000 to set up his own production company.

APPROVED

By 1987 thriving blacksmiths were becoming ever more scarce. 'No Poor Parish' was a series which travelled similar paths to those taken by 'Lesser Spotted Ulster' two decades later.

Back in 1991 Beattie had been in Dublin when he met an RTÉ journalist called Rob Morrison, originally a Belfast man. He had known Morrison in his film editing days. Beattie told him that there was a good job going in UTV if he wanted to return north – editor of 'Counterpoint'.

Rob Morrison had been a seven-year-old in his home in Finaghy on the outskirts of Belfast when he watched 'Robin Hood' on the opening night of UTV. Even then, he was thinking pictures – he thought the opening titles were wonderful. Another decade or so later he was at Warwick University, studying economics. But his interest lay with films, not figures. He enrolled on a two-year course in film and television production at Guildford School of Art, now part of the University for the Creative Arts. From there, he entered BBC Belfast as an assistant film editor. He had always thought he would have a career in the arts but he found himself drawn to current affairs. He was offered a placement in 'Spotlight' as a current affairs producer and that launched his current affairs career. It was consolidated when he made a well-regarded networked documentary on the Kingsmill massacre of ten Protestant workers in South Armagh in January 1976. In 1987, Rob departed for RTÉ, where he worked on 'Today Tonight' and 'Prime Time', winning top journalism awards two years running. He applied for and got the UTV 'Counterpoint' job and two years later was asked to launch 'UTV Live at Six', a new flagship teatime programme.

Morrison privately thought the company was taking something of a risk in appointing a current affairs specialist to the head of an operation encompassing news, but on the other hand, there are those who define current affairs merely as 'long' news. Anyway, 'Live at Six' was to be more than a news programme. It was a programme designed for a post-conflict era, in that it promoted soft features at the top of the programme. It was a bold decision which worried some of the more conservative journalists within UTV, who wondered if a programme which had to have something like the Shankill bombing in its headlines was the right place for softer, fluffier material. What is certain is that the decision to mount such a programme could not have been taken ten years earlier.

UTV 50 YEARS

Presenters Tina Campbell, Paul Clark and Lynda Bryans. Tina became the second female anchor of 'UTV Live' in February 2007 when Kate Smith left.

It was a path UTV had travelled to a degree in times past, using a big-name broadcaster not especially known as a journalist. 'UTV Reports' between 1979 and 1981 was fronted by Gloria Hunniford, in a deliberate move to dilute an unrelieved diet of mayhem. Those were the days when newsroom planning at the beginning of the day was: 'Who's doing the shooting, who the bombing, who the funeral and who the court case?' The old 'UTV Reports' was somewhat different because the editorship of the programme was split. Michael Beattie edited the journalism and a producer looked after the softer material. With 'UTV Live', the buck had one place to stop, whatever the nature of the material, and that was with Morrison. Undoubtedly this was why the company chose someone with Rob Morrison's basket of skills.

He had a strategy. The covering of the conflict had not taken finesse or much presentational craft, just guts and emotional energy and persistence:

> Bread-and-butter issues had never really much of a look-in, but looking back, I don't know if we could have done it any differently. We knew that in the background waiting lists were too long, that there were high levels of dental decay, that we had the highest rates of heart disease, of strokes, of diabetes, of spina bifida – too many highest-rates-of. We covered them, but on the periphery of our agenda and if they got into the running order at all they were doing well. We were obsessed with the Troubles and finding a way out. Ordinary politics were suspended for all those years and we were reflecting that.

> But we had no normal government here, just the Northern Ireland Office. It was staffed by politicians who received no votes here. They were not all that interested in policy other than finding an end to the conflict and an answer to the constitutional problems of the island.

However, the political agenda was slowly changing and that meant the news agenda must follow. It could even be ahead. The new 'UTV Live' had tremendous flexibility. On a hard news day, the news could expand to fill the time available. On a softer day, the news side shrank and features predominated, and having presenters who could handle the range – Mike Nesbitt, Kate Smith, Lynda Bryans, Pamela Ballantine and Paul Clark – was a source of strength.

Morrison deliberately used an attribute of television journalism that is sometimes ignored, discounted or even missed by those dissecting the craft. It is the fact that frequently used television reporters are recognised in the street. 'Recognition has been a cornerstone of our success,' Morrison says. 'This is one of the means we have to achieve an edge. Our people are on every night and this helps recognition. People like Jane Loughrey, Ivan Little or Niall Donnelly. They have a style that is accessible, which helps engender a level of trust in public. When our reporters turn up, the eyewitnesses come to them. By contrast, a BBC reporter who might be from England, or who is not on screen nearly every night, is not immediately recognised and this restricts the flow of people, and therefore of information, towards them. Recognition has been a great help in news gathering.'

Ken Reid, UTV's political editor, is one of the most recognised faces on UTV screens. Reid, originally from Northern Ireland, came to the station from the *Cork Examiner* in 1992, just in time for the run-up to the Good Friday Agreement and other big political changes. Morrison speaks very highly of him: 'Ken has a huge range of contacts, because of his great relationship with all the political parties throughout these islands. When Channel 4's Jon Snow arrives here, his first port of call is Ken. I don't need to worry about politics because Ken is a wonderful political editor.'

However, there were entanglements with government that not even a well-connected political editor could untangle. It is remarkable that, over the thirty years or so journalism of the Troubles, reporters and editors did not clash to any appreciable extent with the D Notice committee, now known as the DA-Notice committee. That is, until right at the very end, when a tussle with UTV threatened to bring down the system which had survived two world wars and a few decades of terrorist war. The DA-Notice system is a voluntary code that provides guidance to British media on the publication or broadcasting of national security information. The aim is to prevent inadvertent disclosure of information that would compromise military and intelligence operations and methods, or risk the safety of those involved in such operations. The system is overseen by the Defence Press and Broadcasting Advisory Committee, a joint government and media body, whose secretary at the time was Rear Admiral Nick Wilkinson. Most journalists in Northern Ireland have never had any dealings with this committee.

UTV made a programme called 'Following Orders', scheduled for broadcast on 24 April 2001, based on revelations from Kevin Fulton – not his real name – who allegedly spied on the IRA on behalf of British forces. Fulton's story was not an issue. The Army was well aware of what he had been saying publicly. The programme dealt more with the general issue of informers. Over a weekend, UTV ran promos telling the audience to watch the programme on the Tuesday evening. The production team knew of the pitfalls in terms of national security and had been at pains to keep the DA-Notice committee aware of the scope of the programme, so was not expecting any last-minute problems. 'We were very straight with them and the committee secretary seemed very appreciative of that,' Morrison said.

That was why Rob Morrison was astounded to receive a telephone call from the Crown Solicitor's office on the morning of transmission, telling him that UTV could not show the programme. Morrison objected and late that afternoon an injunction arrived at Havelock House preventing transmission. The programme had to be pulled from the schedule.

There followed a High Court hearing which required the taking of lengthy affidavits. An Army officer, identified only by the name of Colonel A, supplied the court with evidence on the basis of which the judge said he could not allow the programme to be shown and that the injunction must stand. Colonel A said that if he could see the programme, he would either be reassured or suggest cuts to accommodate his objections. UTV refused to show the programme to military personnel in advance. It would have been an awkward precedent to set.

The issue dragged on over the succeeding months. The court began asking questions about what was to happen. At the next meeting of the DA-Notice committee, Admiral Wilkinson raised the matter. There was a hint that the admiral was not entirely in sympathy with the Ministry of Defence (MOD). Indeed, UTV had found the admiral, as committee secretary, very fair to deal with and had had no complaints about him. The problem was the MOD. Nothing was resolved at this particular meeting, and by the time of the next meeting, the issue had become toxic, with the two sides of the committee at loggerheads. Half the committee consisted of senior media representatives and they were threatening to resign en masse if the issue was not resolved. That sort of standoff was an unprecedented situation within the DA-Notice committee.

Meanwhile UTV were left wondering what on earth in the programme was causing the problem. The committee and the MOD, through the committee, already knew much of what was in the programme. Morrison came to the conclusion that the problem lay with an image in the promo that had been showing the weekend before the programme was due to go out. Somebody in the military had seen something in the promo that had spooked them. But no matter how many times the UTV team looked at the promo, they could see nothing amiss. Not that this mattered. It was what the Army saw – and that was the sticking point.

Not long after the tense committee meeting, a high-level meeting was called at the MOD in London. Alan Bremner, Rob Morrison and 'Insight' editor, Justin O'Brien, flew over to it. The meeting was chaired by a deputy permanent secretary of the MOD, no less, who undermined a fellow MOD civil servant in open session for allowing matters to reach this stage. A compromise was arrived at. Admiral Wilkinson, in his capacity as DA-Notice committee secretary, would watch the programme and if he thought it was fine, it would be transmitted. Shortly after, Admiral Wilkinson came to UTV in Belfast, accompanied by two military intelligence officers. The military intelligence men briefed the admiral. The admiral alone then watched the programme in the UTV boardroom and afterwards conferred privately with the two officers. They emerged at long last, giving the programme the all-clear.

There were two footnotes to the episode. About a year later, Rob Morrison was a guest at a reception hosted by the permanent secretary of the MOD. The two got into conversation. On learning who Morrison was, this very senior civil servant revealed he could hardly believe that a small television company like UTV had rocked the DA-Notice system to such an extent. 'Please tell me it is all sorted,' he said.

On another occasion Morrison was being entertained to dinner at Thiepval Barracks, the military headquarters in Northern Ireland. The man next to Rob suddenly asked, 'Do you know who I am?'

Rob read out the name on the place card. The man smiled and said, 'I am Colonel A.' He then told him that the Army had been genuinely worried that pictures in the film might have revealed an undercover agent. The problem had never been with interviews or the script. To this day, Rob Morrison does not know which pictures – and he will probably never know.

There is only one I.T.V region with nothing shady going on around its borders!

No nightly attacks from the forces of rival I.T.V. regions and their advertising allies. No disruptive guerilla campaigns to upset your carefully planned strategies. The borders of Ulster alone remain free from the ravages of invading aggressors.

So when next you look at all those nasty shaded areas on your map of the regions, look to Northern Ireland. Look at the trouble-free borders of Ulster where you get *real* value for your advertising pound.

Ask M.R. Hutcheson for the details on Northern Ireland — the United Kingdom's only no overlap area.

Ulster Television

 19 MARYLEBONE ROAD · LONDON N.W.1. · Telephone 486-5211

■ UTV advertising itself in the late sixties, trying to identify itself as a good self-contained target marketing area. Interesting caption in the light of history.

191

Chapter 13

The Troubles and how UTV learned to live with them

U TV has over its half-century produced hundreds upon hundreds of worthwhile programmes and it would be tedious within the context of a short history to list them comprehensively. Its news and current affairs have been notably strong, which might be expected since a significant part of the company's history paralleled one of modern Europe's longest periods of paramilitary violence, both internecine and anti-government. Acronyms such as IRA, INLA, UDA and UVF became familiar if not completely understood across much of the developed world as the reportage gained worldwide distribution. In common with the BBC in Belfast, UTV had the unenviable job of fashioning a set of journalistic conventions to allow the reporting of a grim situation which had many similarities to a civil war. The special complication was that it was required to report fighting within a population to that population itself, a role that was particularly sensitive

It is easily forgotten that news about the Troubles was vitally important for large swathes of the population. If a person needed to be out and about, particularly in Belfast, he or she absolutely needed to be aware of the latest happenings. Being knowledgable could make the difference between having your car hijacked or not, or even having your life threatened, simply because an area you had driven through safely in the morning could have become a battlefield by late afternoon. Having said that, by the end of the seventies the management of UTV had discerned an appetite and an audience for programming which was not Troubles-related. An accusation against all news broadcasters at the time was that by concentrating so much on Troubles reporting, what was left of ordinary life was going unreported. The context was being shaded. UTV responded first with the immensely successful 'Good Evening Ulster' programme. It reserved a large section of the programme for soft-news features, even for trivia. Viewers also needed coverage of people going about their ordinary lives, if only as a context for the depressing mayhem.

When Gloria Hunniford left for London and BBC Radio 2 at the end of 1980, there is evidence that UTV was thrown into a state of some confusion. The success of 'Good Evening Ulster' hung on one particular asset, which was its personable, attractive, competent presenter. Of course, good production mattered, but the viewer only saw a face and associated all the good things with that face. They cobbled together a replacement evening programme starting at half past five in the evening, a slot which was interrupted by the ITN news beginning at a quarter to six, returning to UTV at six o'clock. It just didn't work. Its presenters, Gerry Kelly and Gary Gillespie, perhaps unfairly, became associated with the plunge in the audience figures. The programme was reorganised once more, starting at the more sensible time of six o'clock, and it featured a new, fresh face, a 22-year-old called Eamonn Holmes. Like Gloria, he went on to become a national figure and household name.

Gerry Kelly floundered for a period, contemplating leaving UTV for other broadcasters, or even leaving the business altogether. However, he was eventually offered short series chat show formats with programmes like 'Kelly's People', 'Kelly's Eye' and 'Kelly on Tour'. During the 'Kelly's Eye' series, there was a high-profile linkup live with RTÉ's 'Late Late Show', hosted by the doyen of chat

shows, Gay Byrne. The UTV show was actually produced from the RTÉ studio and the UTV management went to Dublin for the occasion. It was successful and probably a turning point in the way in which UTV management viewed chat shows. It must have crossed their minds that if they could get the right vehicle, there was room for such a weekly show from their own studios. Moore Sinnerton, then programme controller, had faith in Kelly, as did Andy Crockart and John McCann. The decision was taken to go with Gerry Kelly and begin a late-evening Friday night chat and entertainment show in mid-September 1989. Naturally there were high hopes, but nobody, not Kelly or anyone in management, could have known that they had pressed the launch button for one of the most successful shows mounted by any of the regional television stations in the United Kingdom, BBC or ITV. The 'Kelly' show became an institution.

The formula was no secret. The 'Late Late' had shown the way clearly for all to see, but that did not in any way guarantee success. After all, Gloria and her

U105's Maurice Jay, Lynda Bryans, Peter McVerry and George Jones, in celebratory mood. UTV set up U105 in Belfast in 2005 as part of its expansion into radio. UTV Media also has stations in Dublin, Cork, Drogheda and Limerick, and sells airtime for a station in Galway.

'Good Evening Ulster' had demonstrated a successful formula, but even the company spawning the programme found difficulty replicating the achievement when Gloria departed the stage. Television is a collaborative process and one factor alone is rarely the golden ingredient, but if a single element is to be isolated as a factor first among equals, it must be the personality, attractiveness and talent of the presenter. A talented presenter can carry lacklustre production for a while, but rarely can talented production carry a presenter without sparkle, without the 'X' factor. Gerry Kelly had it.

But in showbiz, timing is important too, and the 'Kelly' show appeared when the population was ready for what it was offering, which included a showcase for local talent, interviews with celebrities from home and abroad (usually, but not exclusively entertainers), a non-hard-news slant on selected aspects of current affairs, like interviewing Beirut hostage Brian Keenan, followed by reaction with a live studio audience and with the wider audience.

In short, the 'Kelly' show gave Troubles Belfast and its hinterland a taste of what every comparable city and its surroundings in Great Britain and Ireland had been enjoying for decades. Belfast at night, except for a few small areas such as the Great Victoria Street/Dublin Road triangle, was, as the clichéd black-humour observation put it, a graveyard with some streetlights. Theatres, cinemas, nightclubs and restaurants struggled. Some big names, to their credit, did come to Belfast and put on shows, and promoters like Jim Aiken persisted in staging entertainment in conditions which frightened away lesser people. One visiting singer, after an Aiken performance, insisted that the car speeding him away from the venue drove with the boot lid open, so as to prevent a sniper shooting through the rear window – but don't mock. This fearful personage did come, and that is courage. In a small but important way the 'Kelly' programme belongs to the tradition that the show must go on, no matter what. The 'Kelly' show subliminally kept alive for its viewers the prospect of spotlights at the end of the long dark tunnel.

The audience was an important part of the show, and the many who turned up over the years were often amazed at the small size of the studio. Wide angle lenses on the cameras and a skilfully constructed stage set made the whole area seem very much larger than it was. At the time, UTV only had two studios. One was a small news studio and the other was a small general studio, which was used for 'Kelly'. Realistically, putting an audience show into the space available should not have been contemplated, but it was managed by building seating over the scene dock doors (the large doors in the studio wall to admit scenery for the set). This in turn put some of the audience very near the big, bright and hot studio lights needed for the cameras of the time. In all, about a hundred people were squeezed into the space, which left precious little for the performers, including Kelly. (In time, of course, UTV built a bigger studio, which allowed a semi-permanent set for this flagship show. This became a public relations asset because it could also be used for functions, both for hire and for the company itself.)

Furthermore, since the studio was needed for the nightly news programmes, the set had to be built every Friday evening and dismantled afterwards and the news set rebuilt. But it was worth it. Television at the time was still special. There were only a few channels and appearing on television was something singular. The 'Kelly' show deliberately targeted studio audiences from well outside Belfast, something which played very well for the programme and for UTV as a station. It was a night out for people when the opportunities for nights out were limited.

■ UTV Media plc board. *Back row*: Shane Reihill, Helen Kirkpatrick, Jim Downey, Scott Taunton and Norman McKeown. *Front row*: John McCann, group chief executive; John B. McGuckian, chairman; Roy Bailie and Kevin Lagan.

One particular show illustrated attributes which made 'Kelly' a success. It was on Friday 9 February 1996. It was the night that ended the first modern IRA ceasefire after seventeen months, with a huge bomb in the Canary Wharf area of London. In Northern Ireland the mood was one of heartbreak. The ceasefire had seemed to promise so much, only for hope to disappear in the by now familiar TV scenes of death and destruction. Immediately UTV reordered its evening schedule to accommodate special news programmes from its own newsroom and from ITN. The start of the 'Kelly' programme was put back and back, as ad hoc programmes were thrown on air. Gerry Kelly felt the programme should be scrapped, if for no other reason than that he didn't feel like broadcasting a light programme on a dark evening. He said so to Andy Crockart, in charge of programmes. Crockart said the following: 'We've got viewers out there relying on us to keep asserting that there is another world, a better one of smiles and optimism. You go onto that floor and do what you've always done. We especially need to do that on a night like this.'

In his own memoir, *Kelly* (Gill & Macmillan, 2008), Kelly wrote that on this night he really discovered what the old showbiz dictum, 'the show must go on', really meant. He saw that Andy Crockart had been right. The vibes from the studio audience alone told him that it was right. But there might have been another sign. At the time, the 'Kelly' show was playing the 'coin game'. Ten coins were stacked in a column, with heads and tails uppermost, at random. The telephone participant had simply to guess whether each coin would be heads or tails uppermost when uncovered. If the participant got the first coin right, he or she won £50; £100 for the second; £250 for the third and so on. If all ten were guessed correctly, the prize was £25,000. The odds of getting all ten correct are 1,024 to 1. Players could stop and take their winnings at any stage. If they played on and guessed wrongly, they lost everything they had already won.

On this night, a Mr David Donaghy from Lurgan played. Without hesitating, he played every coin correctly up to the ninth, by which point he had won £15,000. He decided, to the utter amazement of all watching that fateful evening, to play the last coin, knowing that if he guessed wrongly he would win nothing.

Choirs of young people have featured throughout the years in UTV programmes. The UTV 'School Choir of the Year' annual series pulled substantial audiences up to the turn of the century.

Mr Donaghy chose correctly. The studio audience erupted, as, probably, did people in homes all over Northern Ireland. Of all the evenings for this to happen! It was an extraordinary moment in the seventeen-year history of the 'Kelly' show, encapsulating in a brief, special instant the exceptional significance of the programme for a beleaguered Northern Ireland.

The last show was on Friday 16 December 2005. It was a heck of a long run. The programme had been a success beyond dreams. As Gerry himself observes, nowadays it would be a miracle to get a seventeen-week run for a programme, never mind seventeen years. However, all things do end and it was probably time to bring down the metaphorical curtain. It was a show born in another television age and it served the company and its audience well, fulfilling and outrunning expectations over an amazing period of time in an industry noted for ephemera. In doing so, the 'Kelly' show became part of television history and rendered Gerry Kelly eligible for induction into the Royal Television Society's Hall of Fame.

Ulster Television's record in serious regional programming stands comparison with the best of ITV companies, big or small. Right from the outset, UTV's serious contributions were being regarded highly by the regulator. Bernard Sendall wrote two seminal volumes of the history of ITV. Sendall was a scholar. At the age of sixteen he won an open scholarship to Magdalen College, Oxford, and at the age of twenty, attained a first-class honours degree in modern history. He had a distinguished career, first in academia, including at Harvard, and then in public service in Britain, ultimately as deputy of the ITA, later the IBA, from 1955 to 1977. It is worth quoting verbatim what Sendall wrote in his second volume (*Independent Television in Britain – Expansion and Change, 1958–1968*) of UTV:

> ... the company's own serious contributions were nearly always enterprising. An outstanding example was the realisation in 1962 of the 'Midnight Oil' project, first mooted by MacQuitty [UTV's inaugural managing director] in 1959. From July 1962 on every weekday evening between 10.40 and 11.15 pm over a period of two months, seven groups of six broadcasts – forty two in all – were given by professors and other members of the teaching staff of Queen's University Belfast. The topics were medicine, law, literature, music, physics, history and economics. Audiences were better than expected. Although the description of 'First

University of the Air' is an excusable exaggeration, such enterprise from a diminutive regional company certainly merited Sir Ivone Kirkpatrick's [Chairman of the ITA 1957–1962] comment, 'a very remarkable effort'. The Authority was sufficiently impressed seriously to contemplate making Northern Ireland the area in which to experiment with the future possibilities of an educational channel.

A year later in July and August 1963, UTV renewed this initiative with another late evening series called 'The Inquiring Mind', giving popular introductions to microbiology, architecture, aviation, music, the visual arts and Ulster's contribution to United States history. By this time, however – since December 1962 – extra broadcasting hours were being allowed by the Post Office (then in charge of UK broadcasting) for approved Adult Education programmes – a fact that makes the earlier 'Midnight Oil' series seem that much more enterprising.

While William MacQuitty takes the accolade for introducing 'Midnight Oil', it was Brum Henderson, MacQuitty's successor as UTV managing director, who picked up this theme of serious programming and ran with it as far as commercial realities would allow. I knew Brum Henderson and was always convinced that when he spoke of the public service obligations laid upon UTV as a condition of their licence to broadcast, he supported them from the heart. He believed public service was a worthwhile obligation, even a privilege. It was he who bought the option on the TV rights for the 'Irish RM' tales by Anglo-Irish novelists, Somerville and Ross, paving the way for a memorable UTV/RTÉ co-produced comedy-drama series based on them, filmed on location in Kildare, Wicklow and the west of Ireland in the 1980s.

UTV even tried single plays, with productions such as 'Boatman do not Tarry' and 'Hidden Curriculum'. They were successful but flashes in the pan. Drama is so expensive that it is realistically beyond the reach of a small regional company. However, UTV has produced over the years documentaries on almost every aspect of life amenable to television – a list which includes religion, farming, cookery, boat-building, history, politics, motorsport, youth, photography, painters, lifestyle and holidays. And much more.

Adrienne Catherwood – McGuill as was – today in her Co. Down home. She is proud of the achievements of her daughter, Andrea Catherwood, who became a notable national and international television reporter.

'Romper Room' was a UTV signature programme for preschool children begun soon after the company started. It was one of the few franchised programmes to appear on any British television and only three ITV companies screened their versions. The UTV version was first hosted by Adrienne McGuill:

[I] think they asked me to do the show because I had hosted a different programme called 'For the Very Young', written by Sheila St Clair. She wrote delightful little stories about Seán the Leprechaun, Danny the Dormouse, Osbert the Owl and so on. Tommy James played the piano and sang children's songs.

When I was doing 'Romper Room', if something went wrong, you covered it as best you could and ploughed on because it was all recorded as live. The only time you would stop and start again was when a light went – you could not broadcast darkness.

A good example was when the floor manager one day signalled 3 minutes to go. So Adrienne asked as a final item if any of the little dears would like to say a poem. One tiny girl volunteered with the following:

> *Way out west where the grass is green*
> *The pussycat sat on a sewing machine*
> *The sewing machine it went so fast*
> *It put six stitches in the pussycat's – ear.*

'I thought for a second that it didn't rhyme – and then I looked round and saw that the crew were laughing themselves silly. I simply said, "That was very good, anyone else?" We had to bleep it out.'

When Adrienne left, Helen Madden took over and in turn also became a household name. But these presenters worked for their money, which was not generous. The five shows to cover the weekdays were recorded, three on a Monday, two the next day, 20 minutes each. 'My car was packed with clothes. I had to have five outfits. I was my own wardrobe mistress,' says Helen. 'I was producing. I organised. There was no secretarial help, but we did have a production assistant on the programme. I had to get the children, get the certificates, get the props. I did everything – for twelve pounds per programme. On my very first day, there was an emergency because one of the little blighters pressed the fire alarm. We had to stop recording and the building was evacuated.'

Towards the end of its run, an odd thing happened in relation to this innocent little programme for infants. In his book, *The Shankill Butchers, the real story of cold-blooded mass murder* (Routledge, 1999), Martin Dillon describes how loyalist killer gangs in Belfast adopted 'Romper Room' as a cover name for the practice of beating up and torturing a victim in front of an audience of associates, usually prior to murdering him hideously. They used the verb 'rompering' to describe the ghastly process, and the usage spread into everyday language during the Troubles, to the horror and mystification of those involved in the programme.

UTV was the first ITV regional company to appoint an environment correspondent, in the person of Brian Black. Brian first made his mark as a reporter for 'Counterpoint', whose high-water mark was in the early 1980s covering politics and violence. There was a special lighter moment when the team was in

Brian Black's perilously close escape at the Magdelena Fjord was captured on film. Huge chunks of the glacier calved into the sea, creating a series of giant waves

Brian Black struggling in the foam. The size of the wave behind him can be judged by scaling it to Brian himself.

Dublin to report on an Anglican synod which was being addressed by Archbishop Tutu. The producer led the great man to where Brian Black and the camera crew were waiting. When he introduced Brian, Tutu began laughing. He was greatly tickled by the idea of being interviewed by a white man called Black.

At the height of the Troubles, Brian became disillusioned with the remorseless grind of the Irish question and made it known to UTV management that his heart lay in reporting upon the environment and the natural world, particularly in Ireland, but also in the cold lands to the north, which he knew to be a barometer of the health of Europe and the world. At first he was providing environment spots within the teatime news programme, but this involved using a precious news camera crew, which curtailed his scope. The solution was for Brian to record the material himself. Luckily, professional technology in the nineties had progressed to the point where the camera could look after exposure and focus automatically, or semi-automatically. UTV trained Brian up and off he went. The result was a freedom to roam and film when he wanted and the results soon proved themselves on screen.

Many will remember his report of a hunted stag which had been driven by the dogs into the sea in Strangford Lough. This was made possible because Brian never

The expression on Brian's face says it all as he stands with his friend James Nixon, having just escaped with his life.

Brian was looking happier when he regained the boat. On the water was better than in the water.

went anywhere without the camera and he came across the terrified, trapped stag by accident. Black also used his expertise as an ocean yachtsman, taking his own boat and crewing on others into the ice-strewn waters of Greenland, Spitzbergen and Iceland, up to around 80° N, to make environmental programmes such as 'Cold Comfort'. It was on one of these trips to the Gullybreen Glacier in Magdelena Fjord that he very nearly lost his life, when huge chunks of the glacier calved into the sea, creating a series of giant waves. Brian was on the shore filming at the time. 'I thought it was goodbye,' he recalls.

> The first huge wave swept me along over the boulders, breaking my backpack strap, ripping the camera away, and dumped me on the shore. The second took me back out to sea into the fjord. I knew not to fight it and did my best to swim with it. Then came the third and I thought this would kill me. These seas contain massive chunks of ice the size of cars. I was now in amongst these and could have been crushed to death. But luckily, with my energy declining, I was dumped on top of rock, which saved my life.

He was bruised and bleeding and three days away from medical help in Reykjavik. 'I flew home from Reykjavik. In Oslo I was waiting for a connection, when Jeannie

Johnston at UTV rang me asking when they could get material. With my arm in sling I told her the story. Remarkably, UTV technicians were able to recover the tape from my battered, sodden camera and we were able to run the pictures.' Even today, one of Brian's hands does not work properly because of the incident, but he continues working. His 'Hidden Heritage' series for UTV has substantial audiences.

UTV's exposition of its own locality is probably best exemplified in the idiosyncratic series, 'Lesser Spotted Ulster', produced and presented by Joe Mahon. Joe Mahon is a Derry man who came into broadcasting through Radio Foyle. He is a consummate wordsmith, historian and folklorist, whose whimsical and very funny verbal essays have been heard in the past on BBC Radio Four. But he has found his home with the 'Lesser Spotted' series, which explores little-known corners of the northern part of the island in a deceptively casual conversational manner, adeptly concealing the great skill required to make this presentational style work seamlessly. It is often watched by almost a third of the whole Northern Ireland television audience. Michael Wilson, UTV's managing director of television says, '"Lesser Spotted Ulster" has been the most watched regional programme in the whole of the ITV network and it has, on occasion, even beaten BBC's soap, "EastEnders". It is a huge success.' Given that Northern Ireland is a soap-addicted audience, this is a major achievement for a programme which is a mixture of history, geography, folklore, geology, biology, climatology, interesting people and wildlife. Plus Joe himself.

The series is in its tenth year and has expanded to be an hour long. It has therefore only seven more years to go to equal the Kelly run. Eight to beat him – that's if Joe Mahon doesn't run out of townlands to visit.

Joe Mahon's 'Lesser Spotted Ulster' programmes have been consistently successful over the years. There are few situations he cannot handle. This might be an exception, if expression and body language are anything to go by.

Chapter 14

From television company to something else

At the beginning of the nineties, the management and directors of Ulster Television huddled tensely around the fax machine just off the boardroom, waiting for it to speak their future like an oracle of old. When it purred into action with a message from the ITC, there was a cheer. They had made it. Their licence had been renewed in the face of competition from two rival groups. But what the company was to achieve over the next dozen or so years was to ensure that its very existence would never depend upon a single fax at a single point in time, giving a single decision from a single source.

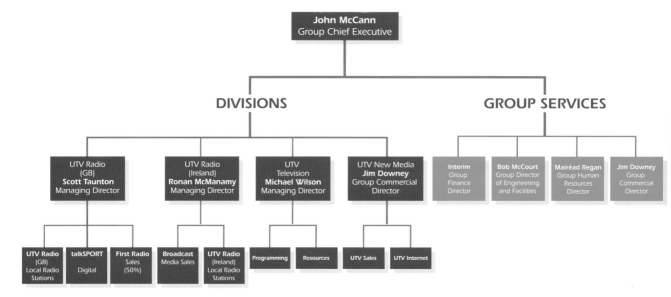

The management structure of UTV Media.

Desmond Smyth as managing director and John McCann as general manager, very much a powerful number two, were a good close-knit team and had decided that they wanted more control – more knowledge, even – in the area of programmes. It was a first target, even before the licence round. Brian Waddell had left and in came Moore Sinnerton. Sinnerton had a commendable background in BBC programming but found the culture in UTV so very different that adjustment was difficult. He left after about a year to become a distinguished independent television producer, but not before he commissioned probably the single most successful series on UTV, the 'Kelly' programme.

After Sinnerton came Maurice Smyth as the new programme head, originally from Northern Ireland but now returning from New Zealand. However, he had been on the other side of the world too long and it soon became apparent that his lack of local knowledge was more than he could speedily make up. The lack of a nose for local places and people, which he recognised himself, made his position uncomfortable, even untenable. An incident involving the long-running motor sport programme, 'RPM', illustrates a reason management needed more control within programmes. The managing director asked one day, 'Where is "RPM" in our schedules?'

1959 - 1999 Turnover

■ TV　　■ New Media　　■ Radio Ireland

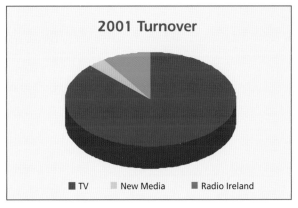

2001 Turnover

■ TV　　■ New Media　　■ Radio Ireland

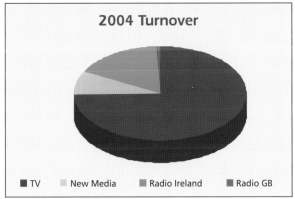

2004 Turnover

■ TV　　■ New Media　　■ Radio Ireland　　■ Radio GB

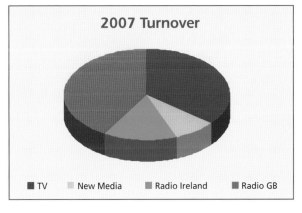

2007 Turnover

■ TV　　■ New Media　　■ Radio Ireland　　■ Radio GB

Comparative UTV turnover through the years.

When he was told that Maurice Smyth had cancelled it, he was aghast, saying it was not to be in the gift of one man to pull a programme like 'RPM' off the airwaves. The programme was reinstated and Maurice Smith returned to the Antipodes to resume a successful career. Alan Bremner took over programmes in 1992 and at last the programme department had the stability it very much needed. Bremner remained in post until retirement in 2006, when Michael Wilson took over.

The nineties were a golden period for Ulster Television. Advertising revenues were buoyant and the programme-makers were given the resources to make a raft of programmes. Rob Morrison had taken a firm hold of the all-important news and current affairs output and the crucial teatime audience soared to new heights. This period saw programmes like 'Lesser Spotted Ulster' begun, new cookery and lifestyle programmes commissioned, the appointment of Brian Black as an environment correspondent. The company was producing far more programming

Turnover

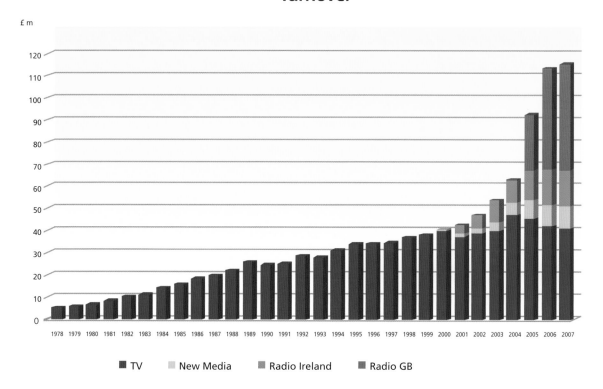

£ m

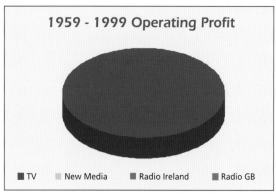

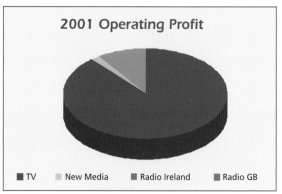

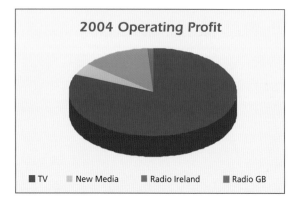

than was required by its contract with the ITC, because it found that local material was very popular, often delivering audience levels well beyond those of network programmes. This made Ulster Television different from most ITV companies in England, where local programmes were often audience losers and were made only to comply with the ITC contract. In fact, the ITV brand was of little value to UTV and they set about supplanting it within on-screen UTV branding. UTV came very near to owning a substantial chunk of TV3, the Republic's first fully commercial terrestrial television station. It was having a troublesome birth. TV3 won the licence to broadcast in 1990 as a consortium including members of U2 and the owner of the Windmill Lane Studios in Dublin. But the station did not appear and the licence was revoked. In 1993 the consortium got it back after court proceedings.

The TV3 project was McCann's first attempt at diversification in the field of television. In the early nineties, he went to see the main shareholders in the consortium, James Morris, Ozzie Kilkenny and U2 manager Paul McGuinness. After a year of tough negotiations, with Desmond Smyth and John McCann going back and forth repeatedly to Dublin, a deal was struck. McCann remembers, 'We signed a deal in the offices of our solicitor in Dublin in St Stephen's Green at four o'clock one morning. That deal gave us eighty per cent and the consortium would own twenty per cent. It was announced at a press conference in the Shelbourne Hotel three hours later.'

But, as sometimes happens with deals, whether in business or elsewhere, when the detail came to be examined and put in place, difficulties surfaced which could not be surmounted. Hence, what could have been a great opportunity for both companies passed by.

Towards the end of the decade, Desmond Smyth and John McCann were together in a car going to a media event in Dublin, when suddenly Smyth turned to McCann and said that he was thinking of retiring. McCann was taken completely by surprise, because Smyth was not yet fifty years of age: 'When Desmond told me he wanted to retire, first of all I did not take him seriously.' Indeed, Desmond Smyth asked John McCann to broach the subject with the company chairman on his behalf and conduct negotiations. This McCann did and in 1999 Desmond Smyth left under very amicable circumstances. He had been managing director since 1983 and in those sixteen years had steered the company with a steady hand through some very turbulent and pressurised times. He had also recruited and struck up a partnership with the man destined to succeed him, to the great benefit of the company. He left the company in a very much stronger position than when he became managing director.

John McCann was now managing director, and the work of diversification began in earnest. With TV3 denied them, UTV now began looking at radio in the Republic of Ireland, as McCann relates: 'I felt that if you understand the marketplace in television, the principles and the selling airtime are similar. I looked at radio in Great Britain and the purchase prices being demanded were too high. So I began looking at Ireland, where the big problem was the ruling of the IRTC, the regulator in Dublin – that you could not own more than twenty-seven per cent of a local radio station. I decided to target Cork, where there were two well-run radio stations owned by the one company.'

The company had been preparing the political ground in the Republic by appearing before two Oireachtas committees on broadcasting and getting people in Dublin accustomed to the notion that UTV was looking south. Then, with some cheek, UTV put together a deal to acquire 100 per cent of the Cork company, and laid it before the IRTC. Unsurprisingly, the regulator pointed to the rule declaring that no one could own more than 27 per cent. UTV asked why such a restriction was in place, which caused some consternation. It certainly was not the reaction the regulator expected. The press got hold of the story, with reporters able to point out that the 27 per cent ownership rule had been circumvented already in Dublin. As the *Sunday Tribune* put it: 'It could be argued that there's little point in having guidelines if you ignore them, while others believe the entire policy on ownership should be scrapped once and for all.'

Conor Maguire, Michael O'Keefe, the IRTC chief executive, John McCann and UTV financial director, Jim Downey met in a hotel at Dublin Airport on a Saturday morning to hammer out an agreement. The IRTC was already worried that the existing ownership rules could be deemed anti-competitive and might be against European Union guidelines. It was a friendly meeting and the parties came to an agreement. UTV could buy 60 per cent of the Cork stations, with an option on the rest of the stock. In the meantime, the whole matter could go to public consultation. In the end, the ownership rules were redrafted to allow 100 per cent

Operating Profit

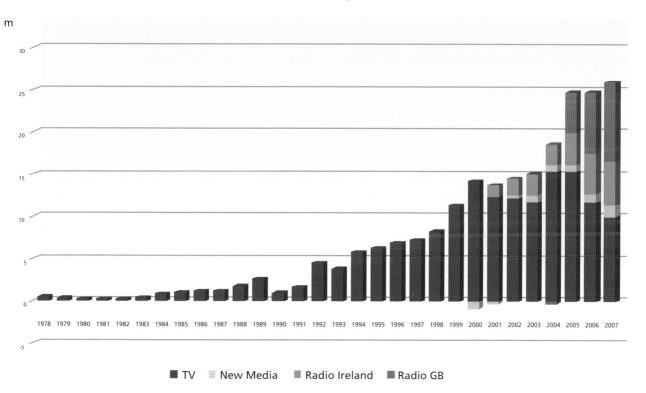

■ TV ■ New Media ■ Radio Ireland ■ Radio GB

Dividends (£m)

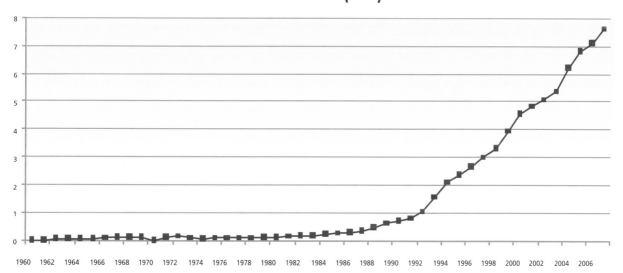

Dividends (£m)

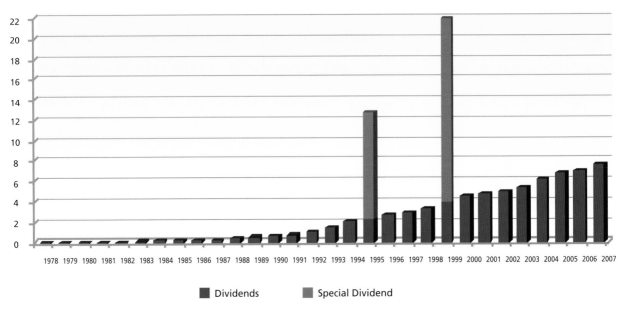

■ Dividends   ■ Special Dividend

Dividends per Share (pence)

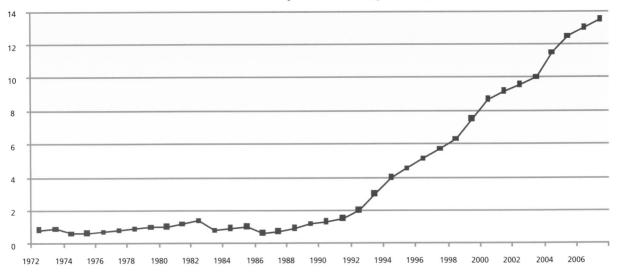

ownership of a radio station. From that initial step, UTV went on to buy two stations in Dublin, where it has about 20 per cent of the market, the largest station in Limerick and the leading stations in Dundalk and Drogheda. It sells the airtime of the Galway station and it has U105 in Belfast. In short, UTV can offer radio advertisers urban advertising over much of Ireland without the expense of also covering sparsely populated rural areas.

The company then began eyeing radio opportunities in Great Britain. At Christmas 2004 it became evident that the Wireless Group was likely to be put up for sale. UTV bought it. There were two elements to the Wireless Group. One was TalkSPORT, a national sport and speech station, and the other was the seventeen radio stations across the United Kingdom. TalkSPORT had clocked up significant losses over a ten-year period, in the region of £75 million. But UTV saw potential in TalkSPORT and thought that it could improve with the local stations as it had done with the Irish stations. The profit being generated by the local stations was being used to compensate for TalkSPORT's losses. The local stations were being starved of cash: they had no investment, no specific market research, no training and no staff development.

When it comes to acquisitions, sometimes the ability to move fast makes all the difference. The UTV board can make big decisions quickly. McCann called Goldman Sachs, who were handling the sale, and put £97 million on the table, saying that UTV could complete with a two-week timeframe. Done! And within another short timeframe, UTV had turned round the Wireless Group from a profit of £3.2 million to about £10 million, eliminating the losses.

I remember having lunch with John McCann and talking about the internet, well before UTV entered the internet provider market. He was interested, but when the Belfast internet provider DNA came on the market, UTV initially missed the event. They entered the fray late, but once more the ability to move fast came into play and they acquired DNA for a shares-plus-cash deal. It was UTV's first diversification. An asset they acquired in the DNA deal providentially was Scott Taunton, one of the principals of DNA. He came across to UTV and was eventually given the Irish radio arm to manage, which he did well. So, when the Wireless Group was bought, Taunton went over to manage. Something similar had happened when UTV had bought the Cork radio stations. Ronan McManamy,

Dividends per Share (pence)

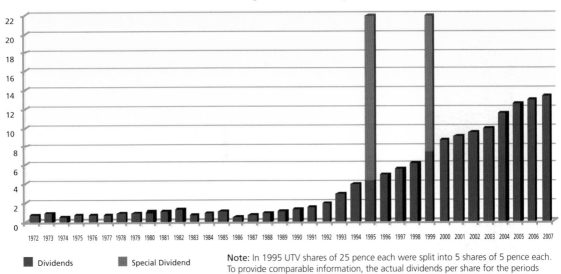

■ Dividends   ▥ Special Dividend

Note: In 1995 UTV shares of 25 pence each were split into 5 shares of 5 pence each. To provide comparable information, the actual dividends per share for the periods prior to 1995 have been divided by 5.

who had been managing director of Cork 96 and 103 FM, became head of all UTV Irish radio stations, including 105 in Belfast.

DNA was rebranded as UTV Internet and expanded to the whole of Ireland, becoming the first in the Republic to offer flat-rate terms. But one thing leads to another. Setting up internet companies requires setting up billing systems, which have similarities with telephony billing systems, and it requires negotiations with telephony companies to buy lines. One day Taunton and McCann were chatting when they realised that they had much of the infrastructure in place to enable them to sell residential telephone services. That they did and yet another arm of business was established. And finally they bought Tibus, a web design and network services company in Belfast.

None of these businesses – Irish radio, GB radio, internet services, web design and telephony, spread over two countries – is vulnerable to a regulator's message declaring they have lost the right to do it. UTV has reinvented itself to the point where, strictly speaking, it is incorrect to describe it as just a television company any longer. It is a media company.

UTV now makes more money from radio than from television and is earning its living from activities impossible even twenty years ago. It has been a long and fascinating journey from that first night of 31 October 1959.

A half-century of both recording history and being part of history.

■ 'Miss Adrienne' using the 'magic' mirror in 'Romper Room' back at the beginning. The magic mirror was a simple device which relied on the imagination of small children for effect. A fitting final image, not just because Adrienne was the first live performer on UTV screens, but because throughout the succeeding half-century, UTV often needed imagination to sustain itself through good times and bad. UTV's service has been a sort of magic mirror reflecting us to ourselves – the superior, the inferior, the invigorating, the saddening, the comical, the illuminating, the depressing, the truthful, the fictional, the damning, and, when circumstances permitted, the inspiring.

Index